SELECTED POEMS
&
POETIC SERIES

SELECTED POEMS
POEMS
&
POETIC
SERIES

THOMAS FINK

MARSH HAWK PRESS
East Rockaway, New York • 2016

Marsh Hawk Press books are published by Poetry Mailing List, Inc., a not-for-profit corporation under section 501 (c) 3 United States Internal Revenue Code.

Cover Painting: Thomas Fink, "Slow Rejoinder 1." 16" × 12". Acrylic on Canvas. 2015.
Author Portrait: Maya D. Mason , "Portrait of Thomas Fink." 30" × 40". Oil on
    Canvas. 2015.
Book Design: Susan Quasha
Text set in Garamond and titles in Minister

Publication of this book was supported by generous grants from the Council of Literary Magazines and Presses via the New York State Council on the Arts

Library of Congress Cataloging-in-Publication Data

Fink, Thomas, 1954- author.
  [Poems. Selections]
  Selected poems and poetic series / Thomas Fink. — First Edition.
      pages cm
  ISBN 978-0-9964275-0-0 (pbk.) — ISBN 0-9964275-0-3 (pbk.)
  I. Title.
  PS3606.I55A6 2015
  811'.6—dc23

                            2015032663

      16 17 18 19.20   7 6 5 4 3 2 1   FIRST EDITION

                    Marsh Hawk Press
                        P.O. Box 206
            East Rockaway, NY 11518-0206
                www.marshhawkpress.org

for Ari and Maya

CONTENTS

Surprise Visit (1993)

Cathartic Choices	3
Minimalist	4
Louise Bourgeois	5
For My Daughter	6
Glass Zone	7
Elite Sands	8

Gossip (2001)

2000	12
Reprise	13
Fingertips	15
Logorrhea	16
Couple	17
Yukiko and Bartleby	18

After Taxes (2004)

Do Dayglo Nights Defile	20
Bootleg Fretwork Pouring	25
Serrated Errors	26
Spin	27
In Memoriam	28
Eel Chord	31
Rice-	32
The Sometime Populists Hesitate	33

No Appointment Necessary (2006)

Responsible Fires Inserted	36
Burrito Imbalance	38
Affable Temblor	39
Could Famines (Hay(Na)Ku/Box)	40

Clarity and Other Poems (2008)

Pyramid Assembled   44
Ralph's Mama   48
When The Ad   51
Departure From A Dead   55
He Wore A Business   56
Monument Odor   57
Alps Bulge.   58
Neigh (Hay[na]ku Exfoliation)   59

Peace Conference (2011)

Vacancy   62
Bid-ness   63
Next Thing You Know   69
Quaint Bombs   70
Burn Reversal   71

Joyride (2013)

How Much Money Do I   74
Burgh's Bloom (Hay(Na)Ku/Box)   76
Syllabus   78
If You & I   80
Spatial Privileges   81
Odd Ditties, Tar Errata   82

New Poems

Who Wet   84
Doppelganger Therapy   85
And See What Happens   86
How Is Your Poodle   87

Series

And Called It Milk   89
Yinglish Strophes   111
Dented Reprise   133
Goad   151
Dusk Bowl Intimacies   173
Home Cooked Diamond   209
Jigsaw Hubbub   221

NOTES AND ACKNOWLEDGMENTS   245
ABOUT THE AUTHOR   247

FROM

Surprise Visit

1993

Cathartic Choices

Enduring
closet guilt?
Quilt it
and burn quickly.

Singled out
for public guilt?
Quilt quickly a
repertoire of quips;
display
most publicly.

If reviled anew,
burn it louder,
as cameras pan.

Should condition persist,
just quit.

Minimalist

handwriting like blush odor
you demand stringent marble

think edge—
square enough empire—
platform atom limn

again tenant shirks
contract—
guess edit perennial—
unsnared equation predicament

swarm interstices

Louise Bourgeois

I fear therefore—
stone

family sleeping
white—white famine

Mother Reason
track your man

inside the cube
I am my own

eyes years
drill questions in the proud cube—
drill to restore

For My Daughter

intimacy chooses—
blood moon
water moon—
delicate night poured

grows you

plenty mouth—
windy howl
storming this sleep
spreading name

Glass Zone

death sugar the boiled
lips renouncing teeth

cut shadow
through needle door
aghast lawn closing heights

dim throat
pleas for psalm juice
darling darling umbrella
or wax

Elite Sands

fireball a thousand peaces

rockeye trolling—
boomer choreography

minimal pain prevail
and quick quick

blitz elite sands—
acrid looting hole ablaze

slit meekly its cities

tornado shield—
vulture rain pillage awash—
chemical light fills the breasts

who (s)oil aqua blame?

foiled skirmish warehouse—
smoke rot backpedaling

guesswork aircraft—
payload air supreme

sadbushwar
deluding embargo—
stammering counter madman—
jubilant rumble whisper death

collateral horrors—
not uncommon fire friend

husband your outcome—
next day bang

precisionguided gunspeak—
no contamination—
electronic debris—legit
bombast fell back to earth

dogfight leaflets—
near starvation base

deprive winter—
would I weep?

won't be home if we don't bomb it

supply route craters—expel the century
what's to mediate?
Patch up limbs—
harass against the air

children who will not wave

Gossip

2001

2000

I'm calling because of the message you left in my dream.
Grapes sagged on the table overnight.

Who founded cottages on paper cliffs and backed off late?

So take the flood insurance out of the wash.

Blowout sages were missing a chip.
Icarus lives, and the sky goes pink.

By all means book me on the next flight,
but leave out the wax.

Reprise

because the night belongs to
money changes every

reflection in the snow-
covered streets of a runaway American

pie drove my
mountain high enough

following you I climb the
face as you were leaving and I'm

about to give you all of my
truth is found to be

like a refugee
and every time you kiss me it's like

another little piece of my
lightning striking again and

a gun over there telling me I've got to
take a walk on the wild

fire I beg you to
give me a ticket for

unconsciousness I'd like to have another
soul who's hit-and-run try to crack some across your

grapevine and I'm just about to lose my
jukebox blowing a fuse hey diddle diddle I'm playing my

diamonds and things right to your
shallow water before I get too

fun fun fun till your daddy
might turn into smoke and I feel ferocious and

claw my way to heaven 'cause I spent my
bed all morning just to pass

the dice it has to be the only
teardrops for one heart to

carry seeds while I was sleeping
in the middle without any plans

sending out an S.O.S.
to the crossroads fell down on my

job in the city working for
five long years I was nothing but your

mother was a tailor she sewed my new
dreams and flying

free why don't you babe get out of my
eyes like windows trickling

human nature why why am I feeling this
very superstitious writing on the

red tail lights heading for
the material world and I am a material

bustle in your hedgerow
throwing shadows on our

prime well didn't you

Fingertips

Actuarial blade:
a gallery of grey screens.

One quits seventeen
times in a single pay
period. No coach

commands the scoreboard if
the despot tranny blows.

Tyranny: this blank check.
Friends are departing

for their own numbers.
What comfort depot?
Don't dun me for a match,
'cause you can launch one from your fingertips.

Sheer will.

Logorrhea

A blind caller knew my name
before I knew the pitch.
Ah, to be pelted with money.
But the hot
and cold signs are screwed on
reversed.
Nerve blizzard.
The much-prepped script
rattles. Too
limbless for escape.

"Employment available.
Inquire within."

Couple

Beige one-
bedroom. Thunderously

high ceiling,
kiddie furniture,

mini-couple.
Much unemployed

square footage,
all vertical.

(Limits to spring
stored

in every set of calves.)
Plastic zeppelins

fizzling.
Perennially

sore necks.
Starving fast.

Yukiko and Bartleby

One likes to let it ring,
to let the dead voice
pick up.
Figures purr aggressively.

Some swoon
for purpose tremors.
I hear a puppy beeping.
It doesn't quite burn.

Are these raisins
or prunes?
They scamper around my immobility.
Who minds the physics of aplomb?

I can prove that you autographed
my copy.
You like everything about me.
Every *thing*.

FROM

After Taxes

2004

Do Dayglo Nights Defile

that gaggle of hinterlands,
your willow campus? Prude
studs, prone to ram

prune accord for a
priapic clambake. Skewers are
hot, eh? Paramilitary collage-
unit to colonize frat
tempo abrasions before orb

taboo calls the wall
and rat tattoos riot
in buff colons. Wobble
gondolas exaggerate smashed supine
bayou syrup. Demented leather
demands of an urn
worse than dearth. Umber

cave hymn or hymnal
goads ace yuppie nostradamus
to drawl sewer-gooped
liturgical pitch. Could cathode
phallus be voted out?
Hug a coast. Knell-
primed jeremiad antics are
nailing thy scars. Our
beams are subject to

rust-fund earl's grouch charity:
staccato errata laying stark ban
dogma on lean pork wages.
Niblick wails at mother nugget.
In lather lab, bald queen
sifts demon diamonds from prosthetic
chastity underwriting milquetoast telos. Boots

up tutu king's tassel hole.
Will mah jong cowpokes pay
a strict, potbellied cake summation
for silk thrust contra sartorial
osteoporosis? Overate, overdosed. That fridge

double-faulted. Evangelical puff-pusch:
groin-free seminar bobbing for
durable rubble. In a sudden

loofah shortage, pogo loam exceeds

forecast. Bugs rally on glam's
past. Model fidos chewing soap
comets till maximum cane vexes

our carp tunnel. Your misery, my
company. Pre-dawn emulsifiers could redistrict
this humble potash portfolio. Bent on
shagging tornado cable, triangular ax exec
sublets flood chord to good bookie

carving arson for insurance bunk rally.
Tax-exempt bigots with mangy corn
grins bid on favorite beards' lymph
shtick. Strategic harlot parleys shrimp bloat
to cap mushroom rages, even if
creek dysfunction spits parson con. Through
smarmed arches, along a milk-lit

cove, john with sabbath lesion is
looping a sybaritic intelligence scarred in
moiré panties. Summer vasectomy series' success
hinging on red chalk's wide ice
screech. Why must a horn-rimmed
accordion tooling in squat car tattle
on b-boys who merely front
backup stake for some "prudent" senate
seed? Peppering scuz snow on barbed

backstreets. Microbe backbeat punning off solid
to crash the pretty. Ever an
additional vortex in fortune's zoo. May
douse with Ritalin but impossible swell
persists. Pins acting saber. Sans toxic
dance bug, we parents can merely
hop to rent rapport. This water's

spoken for. Adequate, at best. New-
agist avenger scavenger loads jutted porno
jugular umbrage into didactic bee pie.
Stardust yo-yo drugging onan skirmish
into a burn-unit samba. Bratwurst

ninja, carwash samurai with smelted
left-field halos crash subway
viola ragas into zebra-toned

Harvard yachts chubby fur, starry

knees, haggard tulips. Wart landowners'
hyper-extended erudition spools forth,
surf eel writing ziplock migraine.

Behind rattlesnake mask, who might
poach elite's opiate élan? Torched
stock pew, tech chattel. If
ostracized, must sack cozy zoning.
Sonorous fund razors pocket whoreson

bacchanalia's borrowed comets toward silt
nostrum. Waste signatories tag landfill
eden. To slit ovarian vest?
Pavilion heist? Come prune atomic
gall's vile gold from the
inverted house's lemon service. Phlegm
lotion shocks. How many birds

skid? Zipper spear. Groin
syntax a personable Tourette's
bullet: short bunt, diesel
gurgle, or electromagnetic vermin
fever. Shrapnel dish of
smeared bipolar faces. Living
on dinosaur sugar, succoring
hellion hussy skin knife,
sprawling vaseline banshee for

pod neighborhood. Valid kiss?
Amiable kick. Column of
recoil colons. Lip me.
Hymen all good acres.
Split persona crumb cake
conks post-macho patriarchy's
nuclear monkey rope. Glow-

worm skates corpuscle patina,
surfing for mojo margin
call. Could any hood's
catatonic tomcat contessa slide
forward to fjord primrose

Versace vinegar toward
more than crystal
self-avenue?

Bootleg Fretwork Pouring

abused rain into yodeling barrel.
Oblivious monocle frugging

to a polyped lagoon's flunking
mammogram. Paradise etchings?
Weather fraud: river's lashed tendons.

Oil horizons spore,
polishing new curs. Moot welkin.
Lacking wholesome dairy
gloss, families mutter ague. Keep

soap alive. In
a gossamer endzone, will a
marigold teaspoon of
homeopathic megilla soothe some acid
engines? A miser's

towels won't dry up mystery
curses. To ban
ulcers: thesis of my soil.
Expand tree roster.
And will this eyeless sun
fold its gun?

Serrated Errors

encrypted in ham. One's
slurred quill slogs through
valium saddlebags. Could we

spiral into some neediness
ward? Spit figure: vertical
armada's snap declaration. Can
a fine ax liberate
harassed vector's pure egg?

Opening what public sense?
As though dice will
go on fiddling till

dotted rats sign out.

Spin

the jewel. That makes

rainbows. Do trees and flies
have bones? Is that water

a boy or a girl? We
had it last night. And
I knew it would come

out of your mouth. This
leaf I keep seeing never
falls down. Must be a
butterfly. The floor could teach

me how to dance. A
world weighs nothing, so how
could it carry all things
in the universe? Don't dare
try to break this wand.

In Memoriam

In those days very few apartments
had air-conditioning. We

sweated it out. Have
you been able to play in
the snow? We spent a quiet
time at home on

New Year's Eve in
deference to our age. We expect
everything to be as expected. Are
you with me? It
was so silent here
in the apartment that I felt

lonely, and then your letter would
arrive. You are not
only a birthday present,
but all that a lucky grandpa
could ever hope for. And in
the next scene of
my dream, we were
all attending your graduation. Is everything

under control? Terrific. May their forehands
improve. Why don't you
put a comb through
your hair? She should not play
tennis until lessons are available. She'll
become unteachable. Move your

feet. Hit it in
the middle. (He looks like Ichabod
Crane.) Everything in moderation. Don't be
a wiseguy, you wiseguy.

Your hair's a rat's
nest. What's the probability of you

getting a shot in the head?
How are you doing
financially? I will not
pay one cent of capital gain

because I don't intend to sell.
I hope we are
around long enough to
provide them with a portfolio that
will have similar success. You follow?
And if you don't,

I do. And that's
what counts because, nevertheless, if you
add it all up, and it
comes out to three,
then that's perfect! If
I get static by Wednesday, then
it must be the circuitry; it
will need repair. I'd

appreciate your guidance in
the area of computers. They hadn't
been invented when I went to
school. Those I met
at camp are still
my closest friends. We are enjoying

our simple daily routines of tennis,
shopping, eating out, etc.
I have been swimming
in the pool that you will

use when you come here. She
is able to draw

such appealing dogs. I
may be prejudiced, but I think you're
terrific. Did you sleep well? Tonight
see how few spots

you can put on
the table. As soon as you're
able to catch and throw a
ball reasonably well, I will buy
you a child's racket. Be sure
that your list consists of things

that will be entertaining, fun to
have. Margaret gave me new batteries
to try. Incidentally, I am impressed
with your telephone manner. Freddy the
Frog says hello and hopes you
had a good Columbus Day in
Las Vegas. You're lucky to have
parents who take you to such

interesting places. Would you like to
climb the rocks on the front
page? Getting back to reality, she
has already stocked the refrigerator. Write
again as soon as you can,
and I promise to answer promptly.

Eel Chord

enough
fluid hokum,
molten dweeb.
Atop berg,
vine diva

davens

steam:

rusting fronds,
sweat lines
on sky
level. Stunned
mica blush.

Rice-

stabilizing green
span aspirin
berates aspiring
sprains and
spartan monad

onus.

For this

portfolio, capital
refrain: long
greenery's immaterial
touch can't
be rusted.

The Sometime Populists Hesitate

to applaud the census. Unmanageable
handwriting. Dubious pedestals remain in
working order. The majority seem/s
enthusiastic about sanctions. And skeptical
of nuclear instructions. It's wise
for us to take the

long way to avert amphibious
traffic. Youth reps mustn't keep
swaggering around conspicuous modesty bastions.
Yet what can stop
a local underside of

pious exertion from popping
off into differently challenged
faces? As long-noggined
experts head for a

collective haircut, I'm ditching
work early to cast
perfumed notes to the

unknown off prodigious cliffs.

FROM

No Appointment Necessary

2006

Responsible Fires Inserted

through quietly funded fringes, under coven of
which patronage hawks hazard avid monitors.
Militant sincerity
invading intel
ligence—
turns to
bureaucratic
blueballs. When
they, sworn warrant
less, fronting we, serve
awe again, we will have squandered the world-
drenched aftermath. Retreat becomes the
keener challenge,
humbly restoring
delay against the
tacitly promised
bilateral sacrifice
momentum. De
lirious "control"
makes it humanly
impossible to go
lightly wrong. The
upper business com
mune asks, "Why
placate the screw
ball executioner's
exegesis?" An auto
crat ally narrowly
blown? Gnat
sledgehammer.
Bright lidded
troops will
serve

yellowcake to typical apartheids. Confederates
distribute redemption grenades to mince jitters.
Al-Qaeda elect
ronic White
House slices
a terrorist
treat. En
trenched trench
metaphors sliding
into his pocket stream.
Preemptive liberty required. Glowing critical
victory pan. This here economy subordinates
that there
varmint en
vironment.
Affordable
wages. We'll
be   planning
for want. How
does the 50
percent slide
out from the
pesticide-laced
elections? Has
a blank check
disarmed the
U.N.? Rogue
hail into the
coffee of their
occupation.

Burrito Imbalance

    lettuce leak. Moths gathering info on youse. No
   aplomb immunity. Fur calls rust.   Sure to flunk
 out of
fashion
school
 before
 matri
    culation. Savings & loan dishing out nuke
    parabolas. Endangered, specious. Can't
                bitchslap
                govern
                ment.
                Won't
                  wave
                    your
                  right to
                  remain
                solvent.
                Side
                walk's a
                Spartan
                bank.

Affable Temblor,

we wanna yearn more.

Mirth telephone

morphine can't

mop up searing

asterisks alone.

Mattress alchemists

are marry

ing around,

but are

they any

less unre

quited? Please

teach twilight

yeomen to nab

wellspring to melt

window wart.

Think about

me when

you masticate.

Could Famines (Hay(Na)Ku/Box)

Could
famines couple?
Girl rows boy
across
alligators. Had
wooed assiduously. They
bunch
damn good.
Spanking curiosity, a
diet
of pearly
obedience. Committee suicide.

You slip into a chance menu. Esperanto imports.
Breathy   hopes
collaborate.   Your
armored   narra
tives, your   ribboned
selves awe   you—
corrobora   tion be
damned—soon to corral another's astonishment.

A
trifle, AWOL,
should not be
misunderestimated.
Office fungus
invests in mercury.
Bowling
with a
pearl. Mink, monkey,
manqué,
minx. The

sport is fidelity.
We're
the ball.
Before honor, think
survival.
Club hemorrhage.
Apology searching for
its
warrant. Rifle
ushers, adolescing late.

FROM

Clarity and Other Poems

2008

Pyramid Assembled

without
overseers.
Waitress trans
mits overtime
depletion to late
patron. The scar could
be masked by ascot, but it
seems contemptuous of anonymity.
However ghosted, chairs on top of the
table permit a last sweep.
Two workers
need a tipless
hour to prep
the café
for bed.
Anyone
up north
disoriented
by high
turnover?
The tipping
of robots is
strictly
inhibited.

In the late
forties, Dad
drove a car
that made
only left
turns.
Underage
thinking
is witnessed
under a convivial
think tank. Hollywood
exposes lessen labor hardships
for the glamorous. Marinated whiplash
backdrop. We impanel the ostensibly
nonaligned.
An off-key
singalong
warms my
malaise.
Cut strings
from the
frame, as
dispro
portionate
empathy or
fright saps
audience
intellection.
It's new,
&   I
recall it
from

adolescence. Billowing, not
bilious. Rapid, not rabid. No
ambidextrous
cars in that
price range
were said to
be available
in that part
of Boston.
What keeps
your fine   capital from
endorsing my chipper burg? One
housefly pings many Senators. Dia
phanous   promises
can get
promis
cuous. A
surefire
klepto
cracy's
high
emissions
emissary
preaches
an enticing
continuum,
but this con
torts contin
gency. Cynical
incision or
cytology?

Globalism by
remote patrol. Hitting
the surnames   a proverbial
urban kilo   meter. I did
not plan   this vacation
to coincide   with a war.
Even if no
school
teaches   you to
turn a   standoff into
an arm   istice, expect a truth
spurt at   amalgam camp. Sustainability,
like a   band saw to   detach phone
from left ear. Con   doms increase
food supply. If   it rains on
this open   tablet, would
                                        its word
                                        motions
                                        concede
                                        to blotting?

Ralph's Mama

couldn't
have
anticipated
a future
common
place of
working
clan   en
durance.
But had
she hushed his ambient
macho & steered him to intricate,
intimate acquaintance with her household
cultivation moves,
Alice could
have extended
her donut
powdering
career. &
then, the
eczema
tinted
tapestry
declaring a
cornucopia
to relieve
the neigh
borhood's
thin slices

would
have
had a
chance
to grow
truer, one
unit at
a time.
Half
century
hence—
TV con
fident it
hasn't run
out of euphoric strategies.
When I peeled the billboard's face,
there was a white x. Are sewers incontinent
by design?
You could
let me
deliver an
undervalued
service
without
sneezing.
Bottom
of a ditch:
"it's not my
fault." He
works the
scales pro-
digiously.
Surprised
at how

tall you haven't
become. Impecunious
bidders catch   the auction's
rhythm.   While de
spising   how, under
the truisms,   prime-time
altruism has
a built-in
meter,   designated
untouch   ables are game
to be   touched. One class's
bleak   argot is found spinning,
mock   jubilant, in   the arse of
another.   We quiz the   left: injection
or insurrection? Vert-   ical for too
long, these chance   parleys must
go way past   laryngitis if
we hope to
encourage
sleetballing
gentrification
to be less
inevitable.

When The Ad

titans
still
flexed
mostly
subterranean
Skinnerian voodoo
with velvet allure, they
venerated gloss, disdained
the unique charm of recycled
tree products. When
a majority of
those with a
pinch of
fortune
were
trained
to over
heat it, to
delete fact,
Times
Square
sported
a randy
neon
mile—
until

the main
grid spat
too often,
& stewards
happened on
the steady,
economical
glow that
oils had supplied
during an earlier
renaissance. Not only
did many resent evidence
that indicts automatic expenditure—
liberty as figure of limitless arms—but,

toward
the jittery
close of
these days,
confirmed
enemies,
fearful
that their
unethical
stocks
would
be cooled,
their vitas
mangled,
collab
orated
to de
fer

obsolescence. As certain am
bition presumed to demand,
they hired
a uniter
who con
formed
instantly
to quick
sand: "I
am just
swallowing   borders." (One
could not be fined for public banality.)
You're too shiny to imagine how, on a
gentrified   patch
of west
ern desert,
psycho
lucidity
from fac
ades &
steel lust
machines
pounded
pried
open
retinas,
but the
casinos'
gradual
nod to
solar is
well

                    documented.   &
                soon, long compulsive
                desires   edged
              gradually   into much
             less decipher   able pulses,
            so the town   came to
           lose its lights
          altogether.
        Texting   Tokyo
       youth, hung   over with
      hedonic nihilism,   decided   one Sun
      day that karaoke hoses had   to flush
         the   pachinko   empire   into the
           ocean. Though no   miracle
             of reversal has   been assur
                                             ed, we must
                                               be rolling
                                                  for   it.

    .

                    —*for Natsuko Hirata*

Departure From A Dead

                    end,
                 sez you,
                  is going
                 to be ex
                 orbitant.
              Indifference
              has been felt as hostility, leading to canards
                 or languorous coexistence without eye con
                                              tact. Ex
                                              clusion
      acts prove un-American. Buzz of   historical
      condescension. A fresh resurgence   of disbelief
                                              in military
                                              solutions
                 might make inclusion acts palatable in
                 some swing states. Can we scratch for
                 rational
                 self de
                 fense
                without
               reaction
              ary budgets?
             Old boy
           imagin
          ation's
         cell isn't
        easy to
       outsmart.

He Wore A Business

and wore business. Primping
prime product. Frock garnishes
wages. A mosquito's misquoting

a simple

blood cache.

Pumped, one pinup prices
& pries & plies
her simpering stumped pimp.

Monument Odor

stresses oblique model of martial
obligations. His overcast motto, mumbled:
omniscient old terms tend good
vines. Schoolyard opening deforms footsteps

toward origin. Toward

treeless threshold? Minus our outer
optics, other topics. Is our
migrant orphaning mutinous mutation or
odds-on hybrid pragmatist manufacture?

Alps Bulge.

Don't budge. Quick
  badges lend a tactical
              radiance.
            A genial
        slap. Caress   of a small,
        infinite rock.   Cult   loads
        balm, shelter.   Sigh thickening.
      Belief, relief.   Is grocery
        anchor   primary?
        The slow   fast was
        pudor's incarnation.
            Don't marry a
          shikse like
          your   cousin
          Mario.   Warp buzz
        of a rote   activist's
      condescend   ing guitar. Tink
      ling.   Bolted   down bulk tempts me
      to bolt. To   seek out an owl, refugee from
      from editor   ial reek. Modesty didn't stop
        him thinking.   Tinkering with
      lightning sway.
      Then wayward
      pontiff doffs
    milky yarmul
  ke, terrifying
  the pious.

Neigh (Hay[na]ku Exfoliation)

Neigh,
I'm your
neighbor. Approach, reproach.

No artifice.
Specializes in the
undemanded. Supply outpaces demand

obscenely. Can this
minimum be absorbed in
the economy? Neighbor: finessed again.

FROM

Peace Conference

2011

Vacancy

Novice. No
vice? No

vase.

No voice?
No vise.

Bid-ness

```
The
Empire
    State                                    Building
      has                                      changed
      colors.                                   Eckert
        & CVS                                   were
          owned                                by the
            same                               mother
            company.                        Depart
                ments        merged;
                  jobs       merged.
                These      are
                working class
                  people     like you
                & me.        Broke up
              his  life.      The market's
          that good?         You  keep
        your person          al  things
          separate            from your
          office.              From "I'm
        getting                 fired," she
        comes                   back  the
      next day                  with "I
    got a raise.                No one
    has gotten                   a  raise
```

63

like this."   So I
  say, "I   don't
   love what   you do;
   I love you."   My com
    pany is be   ing sold.
   I lost my   ticket. Been
    meaning   to leave. I
    should. I   intend to.
    Righto.   With my
     back   ground?
     Come   on! We
     don't want to
    sit back wards.
    You should
    move every 5
    years. It's part
    of the dynamics.
    Your thumb does
   n't stay in the same
   place. There has to
   be an intelligence
  in your thumb. A lot
 of my friends are on
a roller coaster—on so
 many levels. Stupid
numbers: they will never

go away.
  expected
    to people
      no leverage
        it's busy
        You need
        so that the
        comes nat
          It's the
          of the
          the Gulf,
          lifetime
          You'll
          dish
          6 pro
          Chinese
          will be
          Because
          invited to.
          works out
        How much
        forms? Is he
      to go? Raging
     It's been rain
     Brazil since
     ber. Where
       several

                We are
              to sell
             we have
            over. &
           season.
          to work
          pitch be
          ural again.
          sureness
          line. In
        I give
          guarantee.
          be selling
          washers.
          duct ranges.
          & Koreans
           buying.
          we were
          This war
           for us.
           for uni
           excited
            wings.
            ing in
           Decem
           they had
           hundred

women pulling
90% done?
people
been list
interactive
that need
leted. I'm
bring the
of that
meeting
chapter.
see 20
working
what hap
forward.
across
where we
short. I'll
to get to
Radical in
A weed is
you don't
place. I
you're liv
tight area,
ing to pre
capital

down trees.
We saw 3
that hadn't
ening. &
passwords
to be de
going to
outcome
executive
back to the
We want to
people really
on seeing
pens going
Leadership
divisions is
really fall
do our best
the bottom.
what way?
something
want in its
understand
ing in a
but I'm try
serve some
here. Think

Would you
in the middle
When I
seniority
people....
that I've
50, I've
to limit
say. Nia
was the
Truthful
you have
trol, & I
world is
ple who
fast. Too
say to the
"Sorry, I
ply." Why
ways so
out of
be able to
hear the
shapes.
Balanced
by resist

it said "unpaid."
open a mall
of a lake?
have
over
Now
turned
learned
what I
gara Falls
exception.
ly, unless
this con
don't. The
full of peo
can play
many. &
customer,
can't sup
are we al
grossly
step? To

                                            ance. Kinda wanna
                                              get the skinny

from you & see   what I can
    do on my   end. You
       will use   your head to
       steady the   instrument.
       Thanks for   joining. The
       opportunity   we're explor
       ing now is   over at Merck
       with regards   to tablets. He

       took some   thing that ex
       ists & made   it even better
       than it is.   Loaded into
       our test en   vironment.
       Congratula   tions: I've
       never heard   of it, but we
       'll talk about   it when I get
       home. I'll do   what I can
       on the inter
       net first. You
       'll come, &
       it'll be a big
       help. Do I
       what now?
       No one's
       discovered
       this box.

Next Thing You Know

trees
are talking
to Arby.
He's inclined, but
the air is

clogged. "Be as
a tree or a
hill with a will,"
the bed in the

head said. "I be
the shirt here; don't buck
me. Do it, do it,

do it. Be or see."
Is bread inside us? Chance

dances, hair against the wall.

Quaint Bombs

in sleep. Adder on

a ladder.
We have to see

if I
wake up this morning.
The doors

are quick. I'm thinking
about dying.
I don't like the feel
of it.

Burn Reversal

I've been—what—an animal? I

have been since the first time
you met me. When a girl

talks to me, I actually listen,
but my brain is so fantastical.
Her lingo: rivers. Calmly rapturous. "Like

happy and stuff." Motives are
multiple unless otherwise noted. Did
you ever peer at speakers'
facial biceps as they activated

the snow machine? To effect
effect, pressure scale. Shooting
to grow a franchise
until it bursts this
town's straightjacket. By Sunday,

we assume, the
weather will agree.
Do not pass
beyond this
pint without
assistance.

Joyride

2013

How Much Money Do I

have? That's what I thought
I had

when we
started. That money that you
think you have—I couldn't

find it
anywhere. I
want to know where the
money is. He made a

lot of
money once.
Evidently, money is not any
problem. He doesn't need it,
but he

wants to
use it. I spend very
little, and that's what makes
it good
for me.
But I've got more than

that. They're all coming due.
What do
we do—
take our money out? Mine
may be going up, too.
Then why
don't we

claim it? I was thinking
of buying two, three as
he was
talking. I'm
spending the whole thing, because
I really don't do that

much, and
it's well
worth the money. I don't
like her to be so
poor. She

owes her
family a lot of money.
She'll get some—more than
she expected.

Give her
some. I don't know how
much it's gonna cost me.

How much
is it

worth?

Burgh's Bloom (Hay(Na)Ku/Box)

Privately
sectored metropolis:
a prod to
be
remarketed. Gimme
shatterproof tourists, bracket
racket.
Starkest divider
presides, monad dividend
trumping
race (even).
Champagne steamroll. We

with knack for dink in a racial facial and ruddy lion crime ramparts—

to reinstall	a perfect
spurned	town
house.	Endless
ly "not	a politician,"
freed to	mail decis
ions un	clobbered
by millions	angry. Gig
antism's thick	ening bus
iness governs,	out of
torch with the	little fly.
Magi tick: god,	man, sacks
of workforce,	workfierce,
workfarce.	Fewer polite
Titian inter	iors. They're

luring center, rationing periphery. Fjord housing premised? What goes

in
the real?
Net worth bubble
lives
in them.
Compassion? Cares to
be
better, even
if he can't
image
how. Athwart
the needy, the
nerdy.
Tax cute
million heirs not.

Syllabus

Would you consider this

a hard workout? Plastic
shadows. Stealth charmer. Insects

are fond of the
encyclopedia (pages). A responsible
excuse list is circulating.

We can play him.
What a nurse needs to know an
accountant needs? The machine
tells you if something

has to be done.
Don't pay attention; you
must remain unmoved to
stay on top. Disbelief
seduces. Vigor united with
prejudice. Distraction flowers. With brown rice available,

why fill up on
white? Next round, charm
but authority: "Oh, by
the by, you have
to test." A chance
to rage less, be
of desire curious. There

is no plan to move the library.
I shan't crucify you;
it's not in vogue.
What I don't know
is perennial as a
stamp. Balanced, perhaps, on

the tip of an
aside, a small classic
might be opening. When you hear, see,
or smell it, you

intuit, finally, who. Together
is often how. That
raises the quality of

our current. This could
be the song that

keeps her on the bridge.

If You & I

                    sat there &
                 observed for a
              month & a ½ where
          you   sit & nobody talked
        to me. She's the late teller; she
        pushes up fast, fast. Cholo
          diva on warped stilts. If I
            could own that job.
                Comes right behind
                   me & says—I'm not
                    repeating it—"You're
                       walking too slow." The
                          great expert. God in a
                            skirt. Wasn't even his
                              talent. 3 of us asked
                                 him to rotate. The
                                    closer you get to a
                                    full moon, the bigger
                                    an asshole. Blue wall
                             of sirens. Now I need a
                         task order to use the phone—
                      period. If you leave & I
              leave, the same shit's
        gonna happen again.
7 times worse.

Spatial Privileges

Weave of
    blue & bluer
        postcards. Soul
            block. Sustained
                stain. Dosage
                    gamblers have
                fidelity to the
              bigger lice.
          They give
        the min
       imum wag,
        share a fat
        fad, sobering
            bubbly, &
                keep the blood pearl
                    to them
                    selves.
                    "I lust:
                    all   is
                    swell."

Odd Ditties, Tar Errata

Crazy how little moisture we've had. Joyless
hum(or). Canyon burp. Kielbasa cravat. Bearded
gate. Sylph bar with shark

gut upholstery. Grass skirt
affair: faux trot

on

callused lap. Dog
gives you treat. Potable

cake. Impersonally preferred. Putrid gem.
Jet bum. Immaculate ejaculate. A wonderful
poison. Saint? Ain't. Defective—shocking our hands.

New Poems

2014–2015

Who Wet

                    the dream?
     Seduc   tion is
     imbal   ance, as
     every   Saturday
     nightin   gale war
     bles. Sub   tler than
     stupor-   stunted
     pseudo-   studs
     studying   strutting
     strumpets,   set to
     strum. Auto biography's
     drawn from   obscurely
     document   ed lumen
     aries' punts & touch
     downs. The   mechanism
     of their   greatness
     is remote.   While
     romantic   stool
     pigeons   wander
     into one-horse wonderlands

     consummation of amalgama
     tion is   conditioned
     on myopic   focus.
     Notice is   given
     hereby.   Horo
      scopic   surgery
     teaches   them to
      see. We   come in
       tablet   form.
        Gertrude & I are
        still recovering.

Doppelganger Therapy

In closing, I

wish to continue
indefinitely. Sloshed memory

buds. 13 years
since his thorough
disappearance. Only 1

doppelganger (of his
last decade), alone
on Lexington. Silence
facilitating the semblance

job (lest the
voice turn out
alien). Comparable large
round progressive lenses.
Restrained toupee. I
welcome an immediate

response but am
not recognized. Afraid
to try opening
some ghostly dialogue.

Would Pop ever
wear such t-shirt
eyes? Barely possible

whimsy. Breeze wheezes,
creases, freezes. Bread

turns to stone.

And See What Happens

"Sit down in a restaurant and order a tree and see what happens."
—Bill Zavatsky. "The Language Environment." *The Difficulties.* Ed. Tom Beckett.
1.1 (1980) Web. 31 Aug. 2014.

"Words have meaning. And their meaning doesn't change."
—Antonin Scalia. Jennifer Senior. "In Conversation: Antonin Scalia."
New York Magazine. 6 Oct. 2013. Print.

A globe-trotting elephant is carrying a trunk
by the
trunk.
Down the

block is	an establish
ment that	brags they
can trace	roots close
to origins,	yet soon
enough,	you'd see
they're	stumped.
Their	graphic
history	's dead
wood,	won't
nourish	you
branches.	Not
like our	broccoli
special, at	which no
patron	barks. This
time	of year, you

get terrible
apples. Instead,
check out our
pear, peach, bam
boo, or plum
offerings.

How Is Your Poodle

                going to Houston?
The stock   holder
catwalk's   our ex
clusive.   Misprision?
Impossible.   *Managed*
pestilence,   *among other*
factors, lowers   *private costs.*
In our designer chameleon armor, we

're the magnate of magnets for elite op
iate. *Moss*   *& dust*
obscure a   *quiet*
goldmine. If   I can
save a client,   I do—
well, especially   those with
emotional   glass jaws
who never   theless
refrain from   endless
refrains or   affable
eccentrics   who buy a
bus & drive   it to Dela
ware. The   idea that
this lithe   elegance is
varnishing   rape is
another   example of
you pushing   too hard on
the petal, your   rampant ram
part idealism,   which we run
from daily.   So don't
give me   a little
hug. &   watch,
as you   leave the
        gap, for low planes.

And Called It Milk

2001, 2014–2015

And Called It Milk 1

I'm going to stand on my mother,
and it won't hurt
because I'm good.

When Mommy was a little girl,
I was there.
I was in your vagina.
Now I'm the you know what.

Is it cold air on a new face?
Were we crying?

Thank you for giving me a birthday,
my mother. Thank you.

And Called It Milk 2

Maya, you're transmedia looking.
I want you to be a person,
not a messy cloud bag.

You like being a baby?
I want you to grow.

Why are you leaking?
Your sauce is ignorant;
it's spreading
too much everywhere.

Let's hug and kiss Maya
when she climbs my words.

I was out of focus
when it was in her mouth,
but she was trying to talk to the music.

And Called It Milk 3

This day's for sweating.

I wanted to make a river,
but there was a boo boo instead
on that paper.

I'm too young to go alone;
I told you last night.

Gonna make a mistake with my arm.

Because it was my liquid,
I lost control:
yogurt
in the poor bed.

And Called It Milk 4

Food comes from animals.
They must be dying somewhere,
but they're here now.
Now let's have oatmeal
cholesterol.

Cows get hungry after work,
and tigers eat rabbits for breakfast.

Baby grass is drinking
because it has to grow, honey.

When I was a baby,
she fed me
and called it milk.

You tell me less.
But I grew
as I was told.

And Called It Milk 5

You have a body.
(I found it in the wash me machine.)

When does the belly button
become a navel?

Do you have a vagina?
Do you have a banana?

How about the lovely radiator
and all its friends?

Could you take that off to see
how it looks on me?

And Called It Milk 6

The umbilical cord
fell off Maya.

Whoever is standing in my ear:
the idiot
is you.

I can't find my mucous plug.
You better tell your parents that.

Can't tell you about my anger;
have a bagel.

Ennui is funny.
It smells like cucumbers.

My poor pen!
The exclamation
point is gone.

Stupid blue, stupid red.
Stupid is not a color;
it's a word.

Put Maya back in your uterus
now.

And Called It Milk 7

Ruined again:
your big elbow
was like an elevator.

I lost my book in the mud
and broke this arm.

Rotten teeth
fall out of my head.
Many things on the boat of screaming
because we're so asthma.

And you run out from Minaguchi's dangerous
sculpture as the wind
throws its face.

This milk will wake me?
Tastes like Albuterol.
Tylenol.

My mom spoke yes, and I said yes.
She pushed down some buttons and said
bye-bye.

Goodnight ruin;
the leaf is going to sleep in its own place.

And Called It Milk 8

I love Grandpa.
This is a tree.

Are you Daddy?
I'm gonna make your
name. Spell your beard for me again.

Can you please teach me to read
when we get back from the playground?

Are you a pretty jar, Daddy?
You are a discourse.

How's your money
feeling today?

You're an American made out of plastic.

I'm ready for you
to get your paycheck;
money always helps my stomach.

In the fat book,
you taste like a plum.

You're a big fat man,
and that makes me feel better.

And Called It Milk 9

What's above that room?

You were whispering to yourself
like poetry:
the vitamin jar is empty,

and its heart is beating.

I can talk with my lips closed:
Sleep is a new fashion,
and I hardly ever get any.

You know a lot because you have a big brain—
now be quiet.

There are germs in that glass.
Some things
have no shadow because they're invisible.

The butter stained.
It went through the other side.
Now the other side has the same taste.

I'll pick it as quick as your eyes.
Follow my thumb and you'll be there.

And Called It Milk 10

My lip hurts. I
show you in the mirror.

The mirror is bleeding.
See, you crack like this.

Let me see
your beautiful face.

You can see yourself, too,
and also Maya:
a hot pink dress,
the same as mine.

Are we getting pretty now?

My arm is dripping;
I want to have serious hair.

And Called It Milk 11

We're all monsters,
and we all look alike.

"Stop laughing,"
I said to my sister.

She falls down
when I push—
the tyrant baby popcorn brain.

And if it's bad out again,
we'll spank the rain.

And Called It Milk 12

I have two fingers
standing here:
one plus one.

This is my
fantasy:
it's a mouth.

I tasted you
because I was hungry;
you're tasty,
guy.

And Called It Milk 13

Because she doesn't kiss me,
she can't have new shoes.

Welcome to Pavlov Christmas.

Please stop getting presents
at these "great"
second hand stores.

Too many toys,
too much.

We discovered that I was very good.

On their birthday,
all my babies love me.

Stocks, blocks:
they'll have money when they're older.

And Called It Milk 14

Please don't tickle the floor.
(When you do that,
somebody cries.)

Why's my picture
gone?

I don't have blue eyes any more.
Sissie knocked my house down,
and there's no one to like any more.

Trashland.

You can't make chopped
onions all day;
give me a door.

I need you 'cause
there's gonna be a really foul storm.

And Called It Milk 15

That was a good motel,
but now we're home.

Shut up your terribleness now
because we have a sleeping contest.

Sorry.
I can't force you.

What kind of life?
It's resting in the egg.

Is she dead?
Scarab beetle.

And Called It Milk 16

When my teeth leave home,
they'll pass into the moon
and get more bone.
That makes it glowing.

There's only one moon at night
and no shortcut.

Why does the real important news
get shushed?

Today I ate a whole apple
and gave the core to you.

And Called It Milk 17

Count It Higher has a boring face.
He's fascinating;
he doesn't talk.

I take care of that
by making his good-boy life
that bubbles along my video.

His face started to cry
when I gave him candy.

Candy's like a mommy without a brain.

His mother is a statue;
she works a lot.

And Called It Milk 18

See the blue light?
It's my child.

We're spilling the sun of moons, okay?
Playing with eyes.

Moon's walking.
I have to write the moon down:
drawing moon,
drawing one.

And Called It Milk 19

The 7400 bridges
were full of cars.
Must be rubberneck people
losing money. Time.

We can't see their eyes.

And how did you know it was
me in those glasses?
A cinnamon feeling?

Little bird,
come in my invisible home
and try my horse.

And Called It Milk 20

I want an appointment,
but there aren't any dinosaurs around.

All the rocks out here—
Bubbles are made of conscience.

She'd love to wear those stars.

Enough raisins and strawberries—
let me count up to zero.

I try to be a very big mountain,
though we don't know how to burp.

I want to stand
there,
and the moon and the sun help.

Yinglish Strophes

2004, 2006, 2008, 2011, 2013, 2014–2015

Yinglish Strophes 1

I pulled down shade

and that hurted it.
It lays on my
tongue. Four corners. Cavity

spoiling the mouth off.
Is several voids suggested.
I reject. Always a
ladder hard to read.
(A baby can explain

better.) To me it symbolizes.
Bubbles they teaching old-fashionable
drill for boiling us some
reason bulb. That room is
a desperation. The closet is
desperate. That's all I have butter.
I'll taste it how it taste.

Yinglish Strophes 2

Everyone keeps when they go

to war things. You remember
Miss Liberty? Russia's a liar;
I don't believe him. How

far are they? They're in
Cuba. They're slaves. And they
want to expand over the whole
world they want. Not human
people there to give human

rights anyone. I like capitalism.
As far as I remember
is a lot progress. My
dentures isn't Republic or Democratic.
Listen, it's just as bad
all around, and no presidents'll
do any better. To find

meaningful jobs the unemployed. High
cost of living what can
we do about. A great
country like this shouldn't have
their own oil, their own
everything? I have sweet potatoes
don't give me. Soon, soon,
soon, soon you'll get your
steak.

Yinglish Strophes 3

Yesterday was sitting near me

an old man. There's nowhere
such a sunset. Boats, not
much. Very seldom there is

a boat. Ours is only
praying and praying, and he
should forgive us, and we
go out and sin again.
They make a child for

a god. We at least
believe on a ghost. I
haven't got lately, but can't be
bothered now a nice reception. Open
for me all the two doors.
He didn't come yet this Messiah.
I was waiting a long time.

Yinglish Strophes 4

You was four

years living in
dirt and not
good food. Even

a wife if
you'll have—anything
you no good
she says,"Get
the hell out."

But not parents.
So don't forget
that. Not selfish
esteem: wouldn't let
you falling apple
from much that
tree.

Yinglish Strophes 5

The czar,

such czar:
Now I
knew afraid.

My aunt—
hidden out—
and me.
From pogrom
my poor

mother couldn't.
Behind. More word—
never. Do you

stop ever eating?

Yinglish Strophes 6

New York is a lot

of dust. Rice to
a pot boiling: there
goes a dollar thirty-

five. Widow is me.
Deaden. I was myself.
The man told me.
Nothing means to me
anything. I love the air

because I'm used to it.
Eventually once you'll click it.
Just don't despair. Everything good

'll come in your way.

Yinglish Strophes 7

It isn't good. He'll punish me

plenty when I'll come in heaven.
Because we born to Kosher. Don't
seek me why our laws—that's

the Ten Commandments. The other schul—
it wasn't like this so religious.
Even the elevators. You can't touch
Saturday the elevators. It takes you
up; you don't touch. But I'm

not now to gone out rain
and nasty. God allows you that.
God's very good. He's forgiven.

Yinglish Strophes 8

It's a lost

Vegas when they
shovel too shekels
always never stopping

red columns, black
figures. You can't
by me. Sky
my interest. Beautiful,
beautiful, beautiful. We'll

have snow April.
Did you ever
have here April
snow? Do you
remember? Where am
I landing the
next tomorrow is.

Yinglish Strophes 9

So ancient the way

they fight, the way
they kill themselves. She
wouldn't let you anybody

should help her. Home
she didn't: she had
a servant. We really
don't know her money.
By you is more

cheap a little. I'm
not raving like she
does. She likes to
rave. Sometimes friends grow
out you or you
grow out them. Aggressive?
Me? I am still

in a daisy.
Who am I
gonna aggress? It
interferes with talking,
to be togetherness.

Yinglish Strophes 10

Close your chest. Do you

believe in being warm dressed
to your body? Will get
you later arthritis the cold.

Could be chronicle. Yes, yes,
time runs out at you.
The winter is disgusting long.
Why my bones here hurts
me terrible? Now people call

me little. They say I
have bad posture. I used
to have such a good
vision. Even the smallest print
I could read. And wavy
hair. Beautiful wavy. Now like
anything else, no eyes, no

teeth, no hair. Some old
persons, they pitch themselves blonde.
How does blonde come to
a wrinkled face? Oh well,
to bear and grin it.

Yinglish Strophes 11

Unaffordable bread. Stood my

home upside. My father
this 80 years backward
rapid fading. Russian madeleine

doesn't come. You, you
born in English, America
the promise. Can relax
everything know what where
to be it needs.

Bananas gave Island Ellis—
before we never seen.
Outside was bitter tough
to ate but yellow
we did skin. Not
soft white. Ache learns
to stomach.

Yinglish Strophes 12

More you ask me ruggeleh? Cut

the bliss. Don't think it's an
easy job. It's easy to eat
it: one two three. The family

everyone. Guest curious. To go buy
it a few blocks sixty-five
cents. But the folding, heat long
oven—tedious I accept. After even
bitter earth they'll fix me, you'll

have yet six months ruggeleh to
defrosting. Through that snacked already, imitation
store is all: nobody at new

generations know to will achieve.

Yinglish Strophes 13

She's a compulsion eater.

For her, everything was
in her tuchaus. Are
you going for dinner

out? I don't eat there,
don't touch there nothing. For
me's not good whole wheat.
I always said fruit and
vegetables; I think I was

the first one. I had
today a banana. A plum.
For lunch a glass buttermilk.
And two figs. The doctors
when they go to a
meeting all of them, they
eat chicken or fish.

Yinglish Strophes 14

Choir downtown of screeches

doom credit. Loans, was
loans with not even
muscle a few. The

flab full. Unscruples not
down enough the toilet—
vicious papering, not what
produce, not of harvest
nineties of microscope chips.

Yesterday was a nice
movie. Remembered can't your
treasury refurbish. Is second
Roosevelt the Franklin we
obtain? Black now even—
half. Penicillin transparencies should
to every go round.

Yinglish Strophes 15

Through a walls pollute

grizzle. Air condition I
can't so good scrub.
Ah, the greed brain

of smoke industries. Should
build filter to trap the
bad air yet. Their profits
our piles bleed. My husband
he'd puffing secret mostly those

Camels such many years and
a stroke 65. Though almost
90 surprise on medical he
surpass. So people 1950 didn't
linkage the smoked cancer? Not
me education science, but inside
second smoke you smell intelligent.

Yinglish Strophes 16

Benchmarks a crock of 'em,

terrorists monkeying. Harvest full on
refugees stutter generation. Shtetls a
couple they need. Pogrom surging

sectarian this "foundation." Taller democracy
goes every such a moment
young behind her ears. How
good nations reveal violently the
humanitarian (since television). And secure

more? It isn't a helluva
much there. Especial Baghdad to
capitalize. For ally (their alley
blinding) trust gangs security? Extremes
tomorrow dement, demand that same
barrel as you, more decent,
a bargain yet.

Yinglish Strophes 17

– for Stephen Paul Miller

One brother slipped out through

Russian army, me cozy on
the Bronx and my aunt.
Other men the family (we

wasn't communists register) and women
trapped Odessa. Forward 25, those
Nazis didn't concentrate; they killed
immediate not asking. Even Germany
the First War taken revolting

debt treaty, protest yet, but
you should franchise a devil
absolute scourges a whole population
what didn't treaty you? Is
very impossible talk human when
throat furious and mouth pushing
hernia. Jump out history more

60 years: we could
prepare a movie to
their mind the commanders.
Might clearly what disastering
done each sides the
Middle. Shame, long at
the last, for share.
To turn mensch both
two—this can de-escalate.

Yinglish Strophes 18

A million to keep

your promise thanks on
sending. Adorable all day
long the pictures. Dad

is for the real
impatient. There isn't one
millionaire a billionaire enough
dollars to acquire such....
Always hunger? I hope

he has the right
formula. Do not fret
the responsible nerve: she

didn't know neither, Sylvia.

Yinglish Strophes 19

Belmont Portia-- her day

on the races: harsh boobs
bound and wig fright tight,
she an opulent Jew with

floppy a stick bops. Displaced
memsahib could-- if beard cut
or the sideburns lost-- know
him yet? Impersonal any animus?
Wide publishing on bounty endowed

fair Portia. Bassanio's paw manicured
through ample Antonio's pocket up
now a frequent guest. Instead
her papa if Shylock should
be, a muscle pre-nup
would been— plump portion occupying—
into casket the rich lead.

Yinglish Strophes 20

-- for Charles Bernstein and Malcolm Gladwell

Never mind my grammar

ancient can't be vacuumed:
your pants is depressed.
Shouldn't (what to hold

a belt? shirt filth)
comical your age a
schlumper conducting: business is
clothing smooth now, not
that rag sartorial. Skills

to commerce was garments
(general) our Jewish Russian
this liberty nation just

coming and prosper eventual.

Dented Reprise

2004, 2006, 2008, 2011, 2013, 2014–2015

Dented Reprise 1

Debts clank on;

they flood this cot
as our roof is downed—

under flies,
and all the ploy
within you

dries.
Who's booking our indenture
and whatever stuns our bay,
hovel? No blank check

on which we speed.
Stay, blistered lamb.
Yeah, we can
slip a blight's damn lingo.
Please allow me

to reproduce myself
in a pan of stealth
and haste—
to delete the known,
to compete unzoned,
strike a roiling
loan.

Dented Reprise 2

Spaniels are groveling tonight on a chain.

Chew a spike with rabies.
She's a

muscular void,
a discrete, intractable ditty.
She never bought a habit,

and she paints those
gender blinds.
A tether of drizzled pearls
lay a gel on me.

Pee on my pride;
I'll spree on your
slide.
This is no season
to subdivide.

Dented Reprise 3

Below you receive me

with heroic lies.
I know your palaver's

pseudo-tragic
enterprise.
What is that bromide to be brayed?

Why can't you spell me
what you shed?
We're already smitten,
yet today

there'll be a drum
to distemper.
Mojo in a can:
thought you got it strumming,
but it was a druther scam.

Dented Reprise 4

What plots derange our level gaze,

feyly?
Well, the emperor's jiving,

and his beat slits the poor.
Daisy steeple popping,
'cause he's copping some war.

I can't rent no
smattered traction.
Too much donkey isthmus for me
to be dissolved in.

And is it just
raving dream
that could throw
our machine?
And the way you strike

is way beyond a spare.
We've got to brick up
every glitch;
don't free the sleazy, sudsy kitsch.
So give me your art,
make it squeal,
or else infect the doubted.

Dented Reprise 5

Slather

the dirty
fears on e-bay

for blather
on phone oversung.
And if you go

racing Babbits
in an upscale
'burban mall,
dam(n) all the hoopla

croaking chatter filler
and pivot through
the squall.
Go ask phallus
when he's tending
oil.

He'll look at you fright-thighed
and vainly say,
"Am I screwed
if I'm no
longer hung?"
In fealty to our dime,
we cannot tolerate their rind.

The royal tree in our spine
won't exonerate their reduction.
I
will
reply
to this
divide.
We will re-
vive.

Dented Reprise 6

The big-vest charmer's quarters

clearly
snaked appeal all night:

"You stoked my clock
springing eclectic butter.
You got my bole

gleaming an arc."
Guiding my brain
through lion terrain,
sometimes I flare into face,

fear's mal-odor in place.
Who's leaking gout?
Is rapture a crow boat?
Yo, trauma's advance
makes the caddy go block the hole.
Everyone fears rescinding.

Dented Reprise 7

— for Maya

All

beware
of a shove that will skelter

you.
Beware the plumb line
of mere strife.

Bet you're stumbling wanly through
another bland
maze, vaguely blue.
I can tell the way you

clang your bed
that you're a moan now
of bounded lead.
Lay off the pile
upon the Face-
book, a lair, just too

cruel a pub trick.
It is
just dry machination
conning a labored tree.
Just like my hibachi led,
we've gotta keep our
patrons bled.

I could have scolded
you to health;
now let's pound on
someone's wealth.
Bold arm—
I'm plumbing.
Bold dawn—
I'm slumming.

Dented Reprise 8

Bad plans

are endeavored; we're dismayed
when a croaking upstart hands

rubies to the overpaid.
This bummer won't clear with bumming:
warhead count overflow.

Smothered land, better
seed your creds:
step up;
re-route the dead;

drag a home
across the red.
We'll slit a noose today, employ
the means to pluck again
what's been unmade.

Dented Reprise 9

A thin agon, my sahib,

a thicket to pay.
Under my thump,

there's a gland
that once bade me downgrade.
The ghoul that's drooping my magnet

is going AWOL.
Under that thud,
there's a glacier that flushed
me awry.

We've got a tic to rile.
Under my thumbtack,
there's a sly, diseased
cataclysm of a glare.
We've got a tightrope. Too rigid.

Under my thunderclap,
it's the seediest
petrochemical worm.
We've got a tiger to ridicule,
and we don't cave.
My navy don't cave.

Dented Reprise 10

—for Maya

The flock spends a dime

to pose
now.

Facile sly prescription
for a pleasure defection:
the stars, tall, fast,

all plush with dice.
Rumbling in the peon
troves.
That is where

the blues is bre(a)d.
It's a
grey penitentiary box.
Shattered visions,
chilled dens bled.

Wake me,
famished marrow land.
We're gonna shake it maybe if we climb.
Till one's base to grow.
Still one's grace
to flow.

Dented Reprise 11

You keep buyin'

when you ought to be sleuthin'.
Eying little swirls

in plaid. Repent.
Let 'em off. Here's a sweater
from your shelf.

I thought our little aisle climb
had just been fun.
I ain't baiting no
angle of hearsay.

My itches can't try every cling.
But don't—no, don't,
woah, don't
lie to bet yourself cathected.
If you do, you're no better slut for wear.

Dented Reprise 12

When I find myself

in slimy rubble
or sodden prairies' glum decree,

farther than frenzy,
wiping the hurt from my glands
as I balk the depraved,

something in the bay that coos
distracts me like no mother other.
A recession could be turned by this,
so don't let it churn to hell.

Zone me
intuitively;
tone me
till there's spine to gauge
the code we're on.

Dented Reprise 13

Crack bird winging in the dread of white.

Shaken drunken thighs,
infirm of knee,

and the choruses snigger
like rafters.
Help me get my beat back

from the Sound.
Bubbles ahead,
stubble behind,
can't we strew that potion

across barbed lines?
So many different
peepholes to free.
You are only chafing
for this foment to resize.

Dented Reprise 14

What a

yield day for the beak:
carousing frissons

stomp the meek.
It will bring red ramen tide,
make you (sc)ream out,

"Seizure. Fright."
If only we behaved
empirically,
a book

from the wall
unit could
halt the bleeding.
Indolent seasons
might yield to the brain.

Dented Reprise 15

Well, she's grabbed her dazzled carcass

and she's crazin' through the hammer stanza now.
Seems she forgot all about the liberation

like she told her old mandate now,
and with the radius bleeding,
she's crunchin' all the fat in the can: Wow!

And she'll have
fun, funnel, funds
'til the damage takes the t-bill away.
Well, the gunners can't stun 'er

'cause she wars, looms, and drums like an ache now
(you wail like an acid now, you whack like an acorn).
She makes the indulgence of 500
look like a rookie charity racket now
(you lock like an act now, you leak like an ad).

A lot of gumshoes would cathect her,
but she leads 'em to a wildcat gorge chasm now
(you drill like an ague now, you drug like an asp).
And she'll have
function, funk, fungus
'til her daiquiri takes the teammate away.

Goad

2011, 2013, 2014–2015

Goad 1

At 20 &   at 70, I knew the same emotionally stripped

travel   lers. Gunk   impeding their joy faculties & others' on the

            front end   didn't evapor

                  ate on   the back but

                  thicken   ed or spread

                  out to   augment com

                  munal   misery. I al

                  ways lung   ed for their

                  self straight   jacketing

                  non sense.   A razor,

                  tactless? Be   yond a

                  reasonable   clout? I

            was trying to wave.

                  Lost,   lost?

Goad 2

Failure believes in your approach to success: flying
into volcanic ash, window so blasted you can't see past navel
centered lawsuits,
strippers administer
ing bar exams, or
gies of pie in a
blubber patch. Are
you proud to step in
invisible shit? Does mil
dewed torpedo talkathon
bollock tradition underwrite
the license for your sleep
depraved style? Who in hell
could teach your wallet
to sublimate?

Goad 3

An insect played dead in a cup. You rose to squash it.
Human   score cards all over. A wall of dear john letters in a
primrose outhouse. This one
had fallen in love with
the original text,   yet
the person proved a
waste of. Here's to
cake on your sleeve.
Self refilling sophistry keeps
him plugging. Remote con
trol grin. Limber as lumber. So
our purpose in being is to serve
you—specifically? With eter
nity for repayment.

Goad 4

Public blurting   into song is banned in some provinces
due to   coronary   infractions & blushing-for-others suits.
     Here, one   can *kvell*,
     need never   quell the im
     pulse. Your   new acquaint
     ance—owner   of an ocean
     —is generous   to call you "gen
     erous" for "shar   ing" what no
     invisible hand   would caress.

Goad 5

Why insist   on being confused? In ten years, you
could   have no   equity. Cognitive grippe, or bottomless
       grievance?   The wolf
       cries "Boy."   Scar ped
       dled with   out a pinch
       of honor.   Scold me
       tight: when   will you
        pay off your   depths?
            You're doing   nothing. But
               hurting. Yourself.

Goad 6

Enrichment weapons for ecstatic shortcuts. They want
some body for a few weeks. We recognize you from the
picture on the bottle.
Slut of fate? One
whale of an emaciat
ed sign post. Like a
starving waitress
seemingly dispossess
ed of elixir. & not. I
wouldn't want my mystique
rationed. Is cure part of
the service contract?

Goad 7

Genially   attuned to this world as extension of
his art,   his eth   os, his…. Until someone, finding polite
          cowar   dice to be
          ulcer   forming,
          qualifies   the terms
          of his   perfection.
          Enter   the psychic
     guillotine.   & on the
     bus, he   scowls at
      one who   bids him
        (meekly) to   move parcels
       off the neighboring seat.

Goad 8

Maximum   insecurity frisson: might you owe
what   you're   said to own? Dental telepathy pre
       cedes   the root
        call.   "I'll
       never   have
      a wal   nut
      again."   Must
       fund each hole.

Goad 9

The shrike's proud of its volume, tone. Endless smirk
action.   Even the ducks stop their jive at 5. "Aren't you that
actress who pours
beer in her spaghetti?"
Doing it for the signatures?
Why? Your prices are competitive
with major gougers. "Maybe I'll
twist a sale out of her in the
future." Stubborn cancels
affable. Clown quickly
solidifies into ass. In
keeping with the cam
paign for a national reduc
tion in blood   pressure, I hereby
sentence you to 30 seasons of
anyone's lard blabber.

Goad 10

You woke   up to find your garden uprooted. There'd
been   rabid   brown spots on the rhododendron petals &
       floppy,   liquifying
         stems.   The local
         goat   lacks an
       alibi;   its neck
     merits   a fat
      gold   medal,
     but it's   stricken
    past detox.   "Moving?
   An indignity."   After the
execution, I guess you'll buy
more topsoil, seeds.

Goad 11

My dad   used to march here. I have his hat.
Strength   via   AND. Spectacular gains within 2 ½
           gene   rations. The
        grand   objective
    does not   say, "Ex
  cuse me."   Compared
   to which   one is vouch
   safed less than no one.
"Would you care to make
yourself useful?"

Goad 12

"Your   satisfaction is impotent to us." Hearing
protec   tion re   quired beyond this. The harshest corner of
        the per   sonality
        is to be   found
        in that   packet
        of ethics.   Most indel
icate sen   sitivity. The
inner man   ifested by
        teeth. Done   first, ration
        alized soon, bronzed later.

Goad 13

Aghast   prevails. He resents being saddled with anyone
subpar. Intellect   ually, morally. Gum blotches on a sidewalk. Has
           he met   any? Thinks
           so. His   measures?
         Informal,   mercurial.
        Uncodified.   & it's tough
      for those   with ox hubris,
     while walk   ing, to train
   the eyes strai   ght ahead. Go
     on & caress   your anger; I
     will still enjoy my break
          fast tomorrow.

Goad 14

"Take my   keys out of your bag." A bloodthirsty meta
physician's   window   less ethos. Perfecting an echo proof voice. El
         egant   grimace.
       Vintage   vitriol galled
      to tomb   temperature.
      You, im   personal
      friend,   put   acad
       emic   earthquakes
     first. Do   you line the
      pool with   bodies? This
        violence does not impress.

Goad 15

Serf &   sir in necktie tourniquet surfing each surface for
  pleasure   of the next Midas clutch. Whoof. Proof? Poof.
  Bug crawl   ing into a
    tuba.   Charred
   dazzle.   Scalding
  luxuries   squatting
  on brain   machinery.
  Misfortune   500: One
    gets to be a herd.

Goad 16

Matador?   Swinger, splinterer, swindler, predator. "Nearly
  a million   glass jaws nationwide. Potentially, they're all stairs.
   They just   line up
   differently."   Despite
 distribution   require
ments, bak   sheesh
  got your   dogs
   through   Dart
  mouth.   You'll
 never   smell
 like   other
killers or   punch
in a re   morse
code. Some   may not
 be illiterate   translators;
  wait till one   piñata bashes
   back: "How's hell? Satisfied now?"

Goad 17

PAC debate   turns 120. The skinny's already lean, man.
Several winners   climb out of the corpse, congratulate each other,
& (safely distant)   counsel groundlings to
pace their pesos.   Water's sloshing
around in your   former oil wells.
Why are the mar   ket yoyo rampage
econ, liquidity   binges loveable or
livable to you?   Putting a Velcro pad
lock on the   treasury, phallus in blun
derland invited   your pack to splurge from
crisis to crisis,   but that sector had already
invented its own   ass for mooning. Efficiency,
huh? Efficient to   fire folks doing a finer job
of moving product   than the meagre cadre of
successors? Justifiable aplombicide.
Nipping at your tendons.

Goad 18

Snow is   slated for Wednesday: the commerce-busting
kind. Kvetch   marks can't cancel or divert it. Why does their
sour tune seem   productive to
eyes coated with   beer? Keys
hypnotize the   designated
dipso, who talks   elaborately
of the big talker,   dominantly
absent. They think   continually
of those who truly   grate. Which
grates (further). Empathic horse
nods. I hope to nod off.

Goad 19

Your mother   is very loud—of you: "He's been banged
from   Maine   to Bahrain to Brisbane, Sweetie." Some
            suffer   surplus
            while   suppos
        ing they   're graced.
        Perpetual   panic app
        etite?   Many
        pianos   played
            putridly.   Testament
            to growing impotence.

Goad 20

They   give you shot notice: mansion *on* sale. Scheduled
emer   gency.   Bunions to be acquired in paradise. An obscene stench
        of nou   veau drachmas
         in his   chamber as
        he arose.   The loss is
    someone's.   Without
civilized   limits. Re
cognizes   the making
    of monkey?   Engaged to
      be harried,   you mistook
            a name (plate) for gold.

Dusk Bowl Intimacies

2011, 2013, 2014–2015

Dusk Bowl Intimacies 1

My horrible parents just threw me out to the core, like a core. I used
to worship against them. Can evil love deface the file of this life?
I'm not a well-connected martyr and have nothing in my pocket.
Would you like to speak with them about it? If we left in January, it
wouldn't be so frigid.

For
three nights,
we'd eat magnificently.

Dusk Bowl Intimacies 2

All of my husbands were very sweet. The one before had a lovely
voice but left his job, and I sure didn't like him anymore. He wasn't
rich like the others—a poor schlep who didn't seem to study anything
exciting. I bit off a little automobile. This whole place is full of
hookers, and my name is even listed. A lot of women are after the
last one. Closer of a hole. Now he's beginning to try them all. Then
push her off, huh? I decided not to hear about it, then I heard about
it. Is he smarter than we are? You can tell a lot from shoes.

We
don't know
where he's living.
I
have decided
to marry, eventually.

Dusk Bowl Intimacies 3

Who holds the pain? He gave me the words, but I forgot what they were. You're supposed to feed all your –isms that are missing. Can we track them down together? Everyone should own what can never be taken away. As we have no babies to medicate, I mostly think about me.

If
it's soft,
throw it out.

Dusk Bowl Intimacies 4

Here's to all the wonderful people in the world. May many survive—
you especially, my charming brother, who is really my service man.
I wish I was more of a sister to you, like buying us some useful
neighbors. You shouldn't let much stuff leak out of your rectum. Are
we lucky to be lasting so long? Well, my lover-boy Jack's shelter could

keep
us midway
in the pink.

Dusk Bowl Intimacies 5

Nobody's going to tell you something I don't know. Can we throw out the verbiage? We're reading constantly about those who jockey to become very elite intellectually and get stuck in tar. More centrally, where is the food now and where will you send it? To the gun. I need rockets going all

up
and down
in my house.

Dusk Bowl Intimacies 6

My fellow eaters, listen to me and nobody else: leave the table. I
didn't have anything with you. He could have been one of your men
who did window shades. I let him come and lie down, the joy guy.
You can name that my touch of a fog. No one must ever be able

to
snatch it
away from me.

Dusk Bowl Intimacies 7

Swarming charm disarmed, should have alarmed me. A beloved
someone becomes a droop fiend: we forget even who was so
wonderful. Not even married. The little daub I had being attached
to him—he pulled that away. No, I think it's mine. "If you teach,
he'll learn how to feel."

Presuming
a big
spread is hidden.

Dusk Bowl Intimacies 8

"I'm on the scene to coddle the operation. The safe-in-suds standard must be maintained regardless the sacrifice. I trust that my much delayed return has been a source of constant worry to you." It's a matter of nobody knows. You gambled, and I haven't stopped waiting. Don't think I'm guzzling glamor in the meantime.

Good
weather here
means staying inside.

Dusk Bowl Intimacies 9

Why are you worrying about teeth? They'll be dead teeth. I'm careful
about what I buy. We found ourselves—ages ago—strewn together
on a rock. Nowadays Jack favors the candy-striper variety. They're
perky, so I indulge him. I'm really not that much included. Not
complaining—lucky I'm not dead. Those doctors overmedicated
my old chum and practically snuffed her. What can one do with my
leftover to make it joyful? A 5% quick little trip to England? I could
spot a crew of seedy, tweedy visionaries and get endless with them.

Another
year? I'm
not bashed in
yet
because I
have a mind.

Dusk Bowl Intimacies 10

What would you like of me, as if I didn't know? How soon we
forgive. How many dependents now? One guy said, "You don't have
to love her." You have a backside driving you. She hasn't kicked you
out already. They were refugees lining up for the worst medicine,
and she was so execrable to them. Because she tapers down, it's a
nice girlish figure. But who doesn't slump into a slower metabolic....
What's doing with the prices of the equities you are holding? Your
nemesis is acquiring prime acreage in the highlands. Is it a smart
time to close?

And
let crack
punks or premature
heirs
snatch it
away from you.

Dusk Bowl Intimacies 11

The cute little beings, the lovers, yeah—I love their singing. Mind
next to virginal, body not. Crooning aromatherapy into the other's
nostrils. I think they could sit like that for a year. My current
somebody can—blankly. Not on my account. Look at the lovely ears
Joe has.

If
only he
had them tuned.

Dusk Bowl Intimacies 12

Jiff and I contorted. Don't know if he benefited. In his solid days, I think he's been superintendent of some great grammars. But he was getting a little disgusting. So I got rid of Jiff and all his problems. Not about to stare at a guy who is going all the way into the swamp with a fedora on. (So much for mollifying a supreme condo board.) I'll be very sorry if he's losing his mind. Though you can't be homesick at home. You must serve yourself all the time. More and more, that's how the responsible live. If I keep my shoes on,

I
can eat
the next day.
Sylvia,
do you
need a cow?

Dusk Bowl Intimacies 13

This is the year you can kill people. "That's why they ascended?" She was very polite about being murdered. One grandmother who never got it. Then the fancy ones tell you the story that repeats for each. Many times, originally. This is the gallows. You live while you live, and you die while you die. I'm dead now. I died because I had to go certain places. To drop in on my dead, for instance. So far, nobody died of the conundrums I died of. I did almost die once, but I can't really die, so I won't do it too much. When do you expect me to die? I wasn't too thrilled to go, but I am now. Now I know where I stand, so I'm thinking about how to buy the farm. First, I have to get myself a husband. Jake's hanging around until I die.

I
should wanna
conclude about then.
You
can't be
fancy. When I
die,
you can
have these pants.

Dusk Bowl Intimacies 14

Those creamy things, who wants them? They covered my ass,
covered my everything. Waste of distress. Better to grow into a
curable romantic. To wear a thick shawl in that very, very, very cold
place. I'm free at the bottom now.

Our
no-house—
gradually, our fortress.

Dusk Bowl Intimacies 15

Such devastation has been done to me. Everything gets scalloped
up and goes into it. Jack has a child with the woman who stole my
jewelry. The one she purposely made for him. She must have been
way up in the system, as I didn't see her. Now that's an ugly mode
of being—and very slicing. I damned her character. And I even
damned her today, the anniversary of an assassination. She'll make
a miserable wife. Moving away from you slowly. The Chinese food
they served today was everything it said it was going to be. I'll never
be sad again.

Evidently,
my heart's
spectacular. Should he
bolt
from her
and marry me?

Dusk Bowl Intimacies 16

Do you know who died? Practically everybody I care to know. "I'd miss you even if I weren't so damned bored." One person that's cut in half. No book can be written by one person. I'm apt to be dreaming your dreams.

Maybe
I'll give
you a dream.

Dusk Bowl Intimacies 17

Well, anything you buy, you can return within two years. I don't care
if it's gold. There are so many children who look like my lover—
my *ex*-lover. No blame to be blamed here. I won't jump out the
window because that's painful. At one point in the century that's
used up, I was a very pretty mystery who could have done a lot
with a flashbulb or an egg timer. But now it's five or six wars later.
Evidently, Jiff hid many pearls in an unused guitar trunk. I was
supposed to make sure that he was finished. Otherwise, it would be
another $100,000. I was practically shaking hands with the number.
Not married to anyone here.

You
can see
I have two
beds,
and mine's
just lovely now.

Dusk Bowl Intimacies 18

Many times, Jack had to spend money to go to sleep. Longer than
forever, I held out on him. He looks unfinished. The only thing
I like about him is the singing, and he'll hold me to it. We'll buy
a great big coke. Guess I'll unbend, bend down, and give him the
other bag, so why can't we slide into bed, and . . . .

Then
you'll prove
like everybody else.

Dusk Bowl Intimacies 19

I once saw a handsome coven—lovers (by no means, of means)—
up there in the bush, up in the sky. My glasses were alive then.
They want a new religion, too. It isn't just money. For a creed that
won't fold or be stapled. We'll be getting a lot of candidates. My
ex-boyfriend and his brother were deemed dead fish. They brought
them back to life—a couple of days of light. Too late, too early, at
sea. But if you ride on the right horse. . . . Do you ever brush up on
your flying? That's a good strategy to keep me alive a little longer.

Can't
die with
you too far
away.
Otherwise, I'll
die in hell.

Dusk Bowl Intimacies 20

His secretary phoned early to say that he was busy at school. Sticks
to his fibs. I told her that his actions stunk, and I had to know
exactly when he would see me. Think you could ever manage to
hunker down up here where people (famous ones) are now doing all
of those beautiful things? Spotless leather, new silken alloys, plastic
that fools nearly anyone. This has never been ironed. (You can feel
the results.) Still, I wouldn't want to live here if you were never
around. Somebody that really cares about strapping on another
purse, discount-fortified. That sniffs out where bargain side-streets
lie. I'll see if he's really better or not—better for my continuity. Fibs
dry.

And
they crack.
We could lounge
here
until both
of us die.

Dusk Bowl Intimacies 21

I'll get a rash where those flowers are. Digging into me. They'll
be out of control by July. "Shoulda come home last night. There's
roaches in a five-star hotel, too." It had nothing to do with you.
They would fire anyone who walks across their blessed bottom line.
Otiose drudgery that your real mind ejects. What did you think you
would turn out to be? You haven't heard me make a loud, horrible
noise. We call it marriage, but it isn't—for the moment. Let's see
what downhills arise.

I
had as
much when I
started.
What do
you aim for?

Dusk Bowl Intimacies 22

Her children are very boring to me. Is the shrimp adopted? I should care! Jiff told me what he would expect in a wife, and I was not at all thrilled by that—or how many babies that would be. To keep someone busy removing the dust from the morning street. Our current inertia is undefined and suits me indefinitely: we're not unhappy.

And
the guy
believes I'm stunning.

Dusk Bowl Intimacies 23

The widows are always figuring and figuring. It's very tough when
you get involved with any random lug. Sometimes, if he kisses
you, it doesn't mean he likes you: you're there. So don't give it away
because you can use it here or put it where nobody can touch. I
shouldn't have ruined my pictures by showing them to the other
chick. She always has new colors, and I know why. She borrows the
lies, and has a nice billow—if they need a little chicken. My so-called
boyfriend, until today, he's never encountered such love in a roomful
of girls. With the rounded buttocks, which Jewish girls don't
have. Sand is really what they think. As for Jake, he's a workout, a
workload, hole in the blood. I gave him great aspirations, but inside

he's
jelly. An
angel: empty-headed.
You'll
see him—
at my funeral.

Dusk Bowl Intimacies 24

Mother would prop me on her lap, going leedle leedle leedle. This imprint shouldn't have worn off by pimple hour. Everybody in my school—they were all various cheeses. My hands turned funny then, too. Today, we have been organizing our powerhouse. I've been working as a woman about this: do you want

to
unburden yourself
in any way?

Dusk Bowl Intimacies 25

Label everything. If it leaves their body, it should have their full
name on it. We all know what you saw. They shared it with a doctor
and the shoe guy. It's in front of my face when I gimp home, and
I'm just preparing to make my eyes matter. She probably woulda
tried to finish me by now, but I'm not going to be cheated on like
this.

More
than your
imagination. Ultrasonic eyewitness.

Dusk Bowl Intimacies 26

Building a house on a dune! You were sitting on the couch, and you
were kidding? There's really no excuse, though there may have been,
and you've used it somewhere. I'm talking about anybody who's
the least bit considerate of their partner. (Especially knowing my
first injury was that bastard that was going to hit me again—who
bounced from one egg cream to another and sold solid companies
at aggregate loss.) I have

to
put my
feet somewhere, too.

Dusk Bowl Intimacies 27

What happens when somebody like me—an orphan—is living on charity? Abjection stain. They didn't want to keep me overnight like a rotten onion. It's amazing that you found me here. You could have been gone a couple of centuries. I'm not neckless yet so I need my necklace back, please:

for
when my
lack will change.

Dusk Bowl Intimacies 28

Life acts like such a stub, and you should take it. A lot to carry—
but I need you very much. That inconsequential moment when we
realized each other's stain, relived and relived and unrelieved. How
long ago could it have been when I took (myself) to prison? I was
born 92 years ago: senior to anybody in this dustbin. I wasn't too
thrilled before, but I am now. You're a famous person—still a young
man. And I'm very very grateful that you came this particular day
and can't wait to hear about the next whatchamacallit. I really love
you because you have been food to me. Thanks to you, I didn't lose
principal. And interest is steadying again. Let's for the heck of it
check what they have on sale.

No
use in
choking to death.
Enjoy
them for
many, many years.

Dusk Bowl Intimacies 29

He didn't die, trotted out more guts than I have: he came back.
Something to take me out of my little shell. It's too funny, isn't it? I
think I should sleep with him. I didn't and I didn't and I didn't. I'm
practical: a negligible negligee might cheer the sloucher up.

I'd
have to
balm my hands.

Dusk Bowl Intimacies 30

They think you're the doctor? I want a few. They don't even examine
my mouth and see that I really don't live. I'm trying to be cheerful,
though my systems are in error. You can't walk, either? Having to go
every five minutes. A lot of peeing and no place to put it in. They
need gloves to care take of you. Maybe if you act like you belong to
them, you get helped. You only love me and I'm perfect? Who will
look after you? I want to—with all my hearth—

and
I thank
you for that,
feeling
it will
tone me down.

Dusk Bowl Intimacies 31

There's a guy that helps with everything who locked up all my assets.
I didn't even know him and still haven't caught a name. What are
we supposed to do when you tease all these people? Apparently on
her behalf. How does she live? What is she living on? And where
does she get all that old money? I'm infinitely nicer, but she's in
the newspaper. You have cellar rats? She's not interested. Not
interesting, either. Provokes you in every way. I see her children
everywhere. If you make any moves, they're bound to know, too.
She's gonna let you have—? That stinking bitch, a term I won't use
again. But I give you everything. Don't I?

I
get greased
pigeon money, and
you
take the
whole fat stash.
And
you make
"everybody" happy.

Dusk Bowl Intimacies 32

Get out of my throat: the pearls are real, yet no other jewelry
any more—all broken. We realize that I'm not a young lady, that
I expect marriage. Not tulips: roses, if not an upscale nest. Such
a state of socks as I finally got the guy I wanted to marry. Jake is
so manufactured: robot prostate, interior detonator restrained,
retrained. I'm happy to be able.

He's
been showing
me I am.

Dusk Bowl Intimacies 33

Today all the goyim look so goy. I'm afraid of the Italians, with those zaftig revolver sideburns. "I shall be back to collect for another 4 weeks." Use that money to be. A dowry to be ironed out—the modern mode but still sensational. Meanwhile, you can throw me in the corner of any place as long as I'm with my relatives.

Well,
maybe we're
all New Yorkers.

Dusk Bowl Intimacies 34

That isn't my face. I'm an old lady, close to a soup person, and it
doesn't matter. I must have some who-knows-what that people,
when they suddenly glance at me in a room, sometimes like the view.
Jack was looking at me steadily, and he knew quality when he saw
it, as Jiff did hours before. Soon there'll be some present. Both are
dying to sing me.

I
shall not
combine with any.

Dusk Bowl Intimacies 35

Drifters crouch in juntas, going around killing. Can they make their own weather? They did not return the kidneys. Come on—who does that? The courtroom fails: honor's skeleton. Not to look down at anyone, but they should be in a coop where they can control themselves. A behaved beehive. This is the biggest, biggest, biggest, and they ruined a zeitgeist. Do you have all the newspapers? Not right now—but later. I'm interested in having food & friends & a fellow or two I can trust. Joe asked for some liquid, which I thought was important. (His mother takes me in when I get ashamed. Of being.) But I won't. Walk—up a tree? And didn't know until 5:30 what was going on. I feel I'm going to be dying very soon.

Very
important. So
get ready. And
don't
get lazy.
Frolic quickly. Or
you
will never
do it again.

Home Cooked Diamond

2013, 2014–2015

Home Cooked Diamond 1

On the road
to Florida,   birds
are sucked   into
jet engines.   Shoes
hate the   assigned
feet. Earliest   memory:
how dangerous   ly cold it
felt. Despite   the layers
& layers. Snow   field, boy
hunt, thaw.   Didn't get
killed. Thought   that was
lucky. I was   practically
too young   to inform
them. & did   n't, as they
were often
fearful &
homeo sta
sis had
returned.

Home Cooked Diamond 2

                              I am 2 children,
                    the 2 who   are you.
                  This one   eagerly
                    grants   granny her
                    granite   grunt about
                  the gaping   need for
                 strict prag   matism be
                 yond pleasure   schemes.
              Craves capital   continuity
              allot   ments.   Cuts through
                patio patois   with news
                of the mini   scule space
                between tor   ment & ec
               stasy. Knows   when even
                a rock runs   out of time.
               The other trips   regularly ov
               er a reclining bull   in the sky.
              Gets shit on the   hands—or
              something with a   sauce. One
              whose passionate   dining ex
              cludes no treat   group.
              Whose additives   speak
              louder than work   outs &
              addictions louder   than work
              load. Are you   secure? Every
              body should have   a roost where
              they can lasso the   2 into confer
              ence, engineer *a*   *blessing on both*
              your houses. Do   you? Anyway,
            I love this family
            feeling that finds
            me from time
            to time.

Home Cooked Diamond 3

Brood, brooding.
Monitoring   everyone
near. Con   ditioned
to be   stoned on
crisis?   Accused
routinely   of bland
dumb arcs   of blind
ness. *No,*   *they are*
the caricatures: "I'm not
speaking in the   morning
until she makes   me eggs.
So—I love you: do you
have my cat?"   *What you*
do: it's beyond   *valuable.*
The only person   who can
make him feel   human
again. *A gate*   *you're*
not. You   *should*
stop toler
ating…. Let
'em eat kitsch.
From other
kitchens.

Home Cooked Diamond 4

She was more
you than   anybody.
Eyes float   ing, brow
decisive,   chin alert,
hair creep   ing toward
brownblack,   hairline
mobile. Visual   ly you.
This does not,   however,
block a screech   swerve pre
dictable to none   of us. More
than a new tone,   new timing,
new key. Core   vocabulary
that savages   hope of
translation in   to family
idiom. Yet   fully aud
ible, gamb   ling that
mirroring's   sweet
remainder
will coax in
dulgence.

Home Cooked Diamond 5

We did not ask
to see her   privacy
bombing   on screen.
What can   be done
when   the   team time
comes? When   the mort
gaged bedroom   reeks of
penury, when   the friends
are all found   void, we'll
help them with   the money
pot. One cares   to bestow,
but we usually   just give.
Happy if man   aging not
to insult. Do   they sup
pose   that   we love
to conspire?   No more
than Santa,   if he
believes in
children.
We con
spire to
love.

Home Cooked Diamond 6

```
                              Reckless dash
                     for sec        urity?
                  Not just              that.
                Babies to               love
              their moth               ers &
            fathers.                   Were
          you hap                    py for
          them?                     (When
        they got                   up  &
        out.) You                 hardly
      see them.              I  see
      them more.          Where
    I eat— in          all those
      unsung          places. I
      don't          mean
    those. I         mean
  the others.        The
  real ones
who came
with pie.
```

Home Cooked Diamond 7

My mom had 3
husbands.   She kept
the last   name of
a fraud   she was
married   to for
weeks. It   fit, &
he did not.   Yes, Stein
way. He   was just
banging   away on it,
though I   don't know
how much   he practices.
Did you think   I was gonna
buy him a her   itage? A child
makes me self   less?   Never
more than a   few miles out
of my way.   Not doing any
damage. We   didn't have any
bad desserts.   *Do I get my pre*
sent today? You *know how I want*
you to greet me. *Hey, out of my*
purse. She gets   mad because I
call her my seal.   Unfortunately,
she has my hair   line. *Those butter*
flies have little mag   *nets on them. Want*
a strawberry? Ev   eryone's been a
baby once. Cry   ing & yawning
are the best thing.   & I don't want
her in pain. You
're never going
to see those ass
holes. So. Would
you like to be
their   father?

Home Cooked Diamond 8

Nails

are very

odd—

how they

identify.   Where

can I   find my

mother?   She had

to die?   "You were

married   before. I

think you   should be

married   now. We

are ready   to put our

whole off   ice at the

disposal of   having that

conversation."   The whole

thorn for me?   My son, my

son is my song,   is my gong.

My abrasive lamb.   He hung up;

he always does. I'm wondering if

I could walk to his school. *He*

doesn't know you, but he

loves the idea of you.

Home Cooked Diamond 9

```
                          You
                        weren't
                      there for
                    the  dying.
                  Either time.              Close to
                    midnight.               (Best tim
                      ing  for              better en
                    during re               collections,
                    but less                useful for
                  those in                  transition?)
                We're in                    conclusive
              about the                     extent  of
            urn confine                     ment. Some
              pronounce                     ments  had
            been styled                     to stay po
          tent for half                     a century,
        did not. &                          others—like
        how   to                            shave with
        & against                           the grain—
      less  fiercely                        motivated,
        keep returning                      at  crucial
          junctures. They   buck you
            up. Aplomb is had.
```

218

Home Cooked Diamond 10

Can
ancient
skirmishes
be shredded?
Affective
frugality   works
to ebb.   On both
sides.   Geograph
ical re   move is
sometimes   bridged.
A decade's   worth of
no discern   ible discord.
Yet obli   gation baits.
Peer under   the unassum
ing sofa.   Closet sur
renders   sweeping
clause.   "Insincere
service"   punishable
by dearth.   Well design
ed for   post- mor
tem detonation.

Jigsaw Hubbub

2013, 2014–2015

Jigsaw Hubbub 1

Online facts,
burping   forward.
Dreambait?   Jailboat?
You could   put me in
a room with   5 doors, &
I couldn't   find my way
out. I only paid for
the   one   oneness.
The one   we'd hoped
to install   ourselves.
The vacuum   embodies,
they say, a   broad-based
array of pro   duct, seemingly
acrawl with   inner booty &
maximum ass   room. Shadow
competes against   flesh. Dicey
as Eurydice's departure.

Jigsaw Hubbub 2

"I like my pasta
   pure."   She 'd
  close   her eyes
 & eat   slowly,
 soulfully.   A dog
 shat near   the sanc
 tuary. Did   it know?
 Beat this   big rug
  senseless, long as
 it takes. Ashes
 struggle up. Rubble
 spots to   be solved.
Please sit   uncomfort
ably. No   one will win
an invit   ation until
the bath   rooms are
obscenely   clean. Fire
offers a velvet bed. Under a
rubber rain bow, water
moans, "Bullshit."

Jigsaw Hubbub 3

Is the painting
a trickle,   a treatise,
or a cran   ny vista?
A forest   grid?
Water   aflame?
Your mono   cle is
laced with grief:
you fish   only for
the sub   lime. The
kind of   fun that
smarts.   They
wanted   to put a
tuxedo   on the blue
bird, but   her arms
can't fit.   Anyway,
she has a   cruel sun
burn, can   not model
today. & it's   too much
to ask a moon   to drop
a rope ladder.

Jigsaw Hubbub 4

Plaid neighborhood.
I don't   have pants.
By the   way, I
look like   shit in
a costume.   We got
ours at   Dead,
Death, &   Beyond.
Guess who   was supposed
to be captain? Grace
is pudgy.   She's not a
model;   she paid
them. My   genes are
sticking to   me. She
lost around   20, & I
shed about 4.   Yes, I
know moral   enemas
promote cada   verous
aspiration. We'll   do anything
for credit. But   pass me the
oxygen. All   right, thanks:
I might go shopping.

Jigsaw Hubbub 5

                    Gold pajamas
              are yet   pajamas.
              Sunlit   ears. Rad
              iant   fakery. In
              adequate   heavens.
                The scatter   ing of
                  our coinage all
              over "crea   tion." Tender
          unto Caesar   his salad.
      Those book   marked diaries—
    populist,   elitist—excel at
  celebrity.   Upon canon
  ization, the   *sturm und drang*
    obeys its hist   orically tested
      format, & your   search for starker
        inventory goes   hungry. Rain has
          destroyed a water   proof box. Today's
            special could be   an imperm; please
                hold the chemicals.

Jigsaw Hubbub 6

She really likes
anesthesia?   Is that
wrong?   Submits
material   to cover
girl anon   ymity.
Blankets   without
fringe are   whip-
stitched. Belt.
Discipline.   "Spirit"
acquired   via basic
writhing.   Gauze of
sweat de   votion. Sap in
tail? None   to envision.
Impossible   lips—terribly
white. Privi   lege of un
natural hair.   Doesn't re
semble any   known hu
man lump.   Corn in the
clouds. So   what if actual
bloom is   underneath:
who peers   there? & now
we'll see her all the livelong night.

Jigsaw Hubbub 7

Lubricated gnats
in necktie   tourniquets
glut the   treadway.
A few note   the white-
gloved   Tokyo de
partment   store ele
vator girls,   who may
be the politest beings
above   ground.
Are the   gals paid
enough   for sinking
(as it   seems from
the out   side) into
reiterative   self loss?
Without dying.   In the mini
mum security   of a   rabbit hutch,
does their mir   ror's ice melt?
One gnat is sud   denly conscious
of how his swash   buckling ego is
ravaging his liver,   his intestines. If
the gals knew he'd   be appropriating
some of their alleged   surfaces for self re
juvenation, would they crack up— as if
witnessing a cucumber explode?

Jigsaw Hubbub 8

Claiming to de
liver a   whiff of
epicenter,   illiterate
translators   recruit
fresh   placebo
addicts.   See bards
drifting from
communion   to com
munion,   searching
the moon   for a beat,
cruising   earnestly
for vision.   One blows
a whiff up   to poster size.
Well, that's   wonderful,
but it doesn't   last. Fat fad
of the unnamable.

Jigsaw Hubbub 9

The family coalesced.
Around a   *narcotic*
technology.   You re
sound   with   doves;
I prefer   un   natural
light. So   lost
without   my cell.
Not ador   able—dan
gerous. *Ah, for the*
love of   *ubiquity!*
Has the   *equipment*
been de   *signed for*
your   *maturity*
level?   Not
gonna   punch
in the   remorse
code today.   It's a
schlumpy   gestalt,
Jethro. *Wisdom*   *won't fit*
on that button.   Your aph
orisms (dust bin   of an abso
lute) distract me   from my
primal jones: glid   ing from Point
D to Point Q to Point N.

Jigsaw Hubbub 10

                        The hangman,
            taciturn   at twilight,
            doubles   as a greg
            arious   accountant
            by day.   Tell me who
              your mother   was in the
                  class picture. (She's still
            12 in my   eyes.) It tries
          to announce: "I'm matter:
          believe."   Stronger than
          dearth.   But the onstage
        struggle   against   sunset bumps
      into ashes   in a pail. That
      huge self   fits in a dopp
      kit. Remain   der: reminder
        that   some   things just are.
        A laugh to   break vases. Say
          ing goodbye   the whole con
            versation? In   ternal weeding
              is the prelim.   It will be an
                incredible conference final.

Jigsaw Hubbub 11

Can momentous
beginning   be forever?
Someone   sticks his
head   out of a
train   window;
a tree   axes   it. An
other is   hitched
beneath rifle blos
som. No   eros without
the unsure.   Intimate with
contamin   ants? She
wouldn't   relinquish
this car   diac   release
for a   clam's
calm.   But
when   does an
organized   retreat
prove our   best foot
forward? Just   not just now.
Dad, I promise   not to lose any
more companies.

Jigsaw Hubbub 12

Spiritual's immaterial.
You gotta   train the
mind stead   ily on sur
vival. To   survive.
During   this long
downdrift,   we were
asked to   nibble back
on some   prunes. Com
plied. To capture gross
cost savings,   long term
efficiency   hangs on out
sourcing   relationships &
division-   specific accelera
tion of   discipline amid
industry   headwinds. Big
boutiques   are   short on research
today, but   slow steady grow
ers still sport   a bit of a floor
to them. Pro   gress   is trying to speak
in hic cups.   Granted that the
digestion pro   cess is strenuous
on orphans   & widows. So streng
then your   stomach with growth
drivers & run them in parallel.

Jigsaw Hubbub 13

Desperately respectable,
vulnerable   sledgehammers
milk their   predilection
for divine   sword.
They sense   that the
well-nourished   specter in
their drug attic favors
them with   an inverted
breeze.   Their charge
is the flip   side of a
testosterone   bender.
Your god   *could grad*
ually run   *out of team.*
May that   *ground floor*
window open   *when it feels*
right to jump out.

Jigsaw Hubbub 14

                    The boys are sold
          on the   same starry
          story: *All's ya*
     need is   *a laptop,*
     sunglasses,   *& a car.*
          Someday,   they'll
             trip over   the epi
             phany that one
        is expected   to supply
        content.   Meantime,
     in a distant   precinct of
     proverbia,   the overexam
     ined ex   istence
groans—   a pitchfork
in thought's   neck, a twi
light rendez   vous with an
     invisible trap   door.   Even
     psychologists   hatched from
        a crisis creek   might concur
        that incontinent   motif reiteration
          is devil therapy.   I will not address the
             shadows. Please spray   the boulder with mist
          so that the beautiful lichen continues to thrive.

Jigsaw Hubbub 15

Who touched me
down   there?
Efficien   cy   Gestapo
hails   "section-
based   credential
ing"   as   "overture
to the   beauty to
come." Sometimes,
rain works   methodically
across a   tough dust
strip. But   hell can
dwell in   fierce ex
ternals.   Hear those
italics   whisper?
Death is   lost   on the cred
entialing   enthusers &
their smooth   guru. Will catch
up. Wax offer to follow.

Jigsaw Hubbub 16

She feels like *a*

permanent   *extra,* as

though   lodged, an

afterthought,   in a rusty

clapboard af   fair squatting

in gray tulips,   where sunshine

doesn't shine, & the

cat is bigger   than the child.

No perfume   of kindness.

Breast milk: *essentialist*

at best. He   *sent his*

mother home.   *I want to*

know who my   *people are.*

A wish to stay   underwater—

until we are   ready to put

our whole office   at the disposal

of that conversation.

Jigsaw Hubbub 17

I think I'm the
richest   person
in this   subway
car. *Does*   *it*   *wear off?*
You bet.   Once,
when the   Great
Depression was my
sole pro   fessor,
it was   heaven
to be   bored.
Lately,   I'm   too much
the maestro   of prere
corded fun.   To each
skinflint blood   stream his
phone. Inhuman   resources.
Crossing the   avenue? Get
me anything they don't have.

Jigsaw Hubbub 18

Assume the
position.　　　Goal of
　　a sleeker　　　　　jail.
　　Crushed　　　　flesh
　　　here.　　　Prime
　　　risk: a facile
　　farce　　　arising
　out of　　　　　　the torn
rose of　　　　　　　　a face?
Faceheft　　bu(o)ys　　　　a glorious
alias.　　　　No　　　　　creases
in the　　　　　　　　　thesis.
　Perfumed　　　bones.　　　Choice
　　carcinogens　　　embedded.
　　Nervous narcissus rhapsody.

Jigsaw Hubbub 19

"Let's pretend we're real

   human   leather."

The thrill   kept   pump

ing for a   week;

you were   vexed   to lose

it. Eventual   return?

Perhaps after   a long

series of baths.

"But you   can see

that my   purchase

was a big   success, &

if anything   dares be

grime it,   I will

have to   go out

& buy   another,"

since col   lection   (here) assumes

agency; in   the desert, there

's no ATM.   A scarf unwinds

on the windy vista.

Jigsaw Hubbub 20

                You can hang
            this right   now. Where
        did you   buy it?
          & what   does   that
            make it?   Splash
              of class? Una
          shamedly   harmonious.
        Reason to   boycott
      despair?   See what
    you want   it to be.
      Everything   here.
          Imagine that.   Exists,
                exits. Immensity again.

Jigsaw Hubbub 21

Temperance
leaflets   sloshed
beside   a keg.
Sheet   rock
holo   gram's
doodle dance.
"They   gave me
all the   money
back—   every fuck
in' dime."   The house
lowers the   sound track
for this con   vulsion.
Available night   ly, akin to
generic climax.   Militant
mutilation of the formless.

Jigsaw Hubbub 22

Complacency is rotten
for the per   petually com
placent &,   more so, for
the ones   who suffer
them. Yet   those whose
habitual facial   mode is "just
been punched"   could use a
touch of that.   Dried flood.
Collarbone cobra. Unsus
tainable weight.   No coating
will survive   forever out
doors. Who   might be the
CEO of   their   nervous system?
Frozen into   flinch. Rifling
through a   nearly inex
haustible store   of sense
ma(s)king strategies,   we lack a
narrative crutch, crotch.   Some know what
they want to play but can't   find the birds. Almost
ready to join United Orb Hurlers against Gravity.

Jigsaw Hubbub 23

In Hollywood &
elsewhere,   waterless
urinals   shave
off up   to 45
gallons   of   flush
per annum.   30 years
ago, you   could
fix a car; now you
have to   consult it
about how   it wants to
be fixed.   Hope they
put in   plenty of
what if.   Mislay a
single   quotidian
detail, &   the software
in question   metallically   announces:
You are behind   *this. We know*
how to scoop you   *up.* If they're
looking for some   milquetoast
to play deadbeat   greeting the
eternal nightstick,   they'd best
keep scrolling. War   still gnaws on
foundations: why   isn't our brilliant
new electronic sove   reign ready with
virtual pacifiers? Why   can't it whip up a
million careers in earthquake prevention?

Notes and Acknowledgments

Grateful acknowledgment is made to the following publications where poems included in prior books appeared, sometimes in different versions and, very occasionally, with different titles: *Ambit, Anti-, Aught, Barrow Street, BlazeVox, Blue and Yellow Dog, Community Review, Cricket Online Review, Critiphoria, Diode, Eratio Postmodern Poetry, Fieralingue, In Transit, Locus Point, Long Island Quarterly, Marsh Hawk Review, Milk, Moria, New Observations, Of(f)course, Otoliths, Poetry New York, Rife, Second Avenue, Shampoo, Shofar, Skanky Possum, Press 1, Raft, Swirl, Talisman, Tin Lustre Mobile, Word For/ Word, x-Stream.*

Grateful acknowledgment is made to the following publications where new poems have appeared: *Marsh Hawk Review:* "And See What Happens" (formerly titled "Airtight Cognition"); *Otoliths:* "Dusk Bowl Intimacies 20" (formerly 40); *Ping-Pong:* "Dented Reprise 14; *Set:* "Goad 3" (formerly 33).

The term "Yinglish," coined by Leo J. Rosten, indicates Yiddish syntax imported into English.

Various poems published in previous books that were part of a series included in this collection have been revised or eliminated, and some new poems have been added. Therefore, in a given series in this volume, the numbers of particular poems have been changed.

About the Author

Thomas Fink, born in New York City in 1954, is the author of eight previous books of poetry—most recently, *Joyride* (2013). He has authored two books of criticism, including *"A Different Sense of Power": Problems of Community in Late-Twentieth Century U.S. Poetry* (Fairleigh Dickinson University Press, 2001), and has co-edited two collections of criticism, including *Reading the Difficulties: Dialogues with Contemporary American Innovative Poetry* (University of Alabama Press, 2014). His poem, "Yinglish Strophes 9," was selected for *The Best American Poetry 2007* (Scribner's) by Heather McHugh and David Lehman. His paintings hang in various collections. Fink is Professor of English at City University of New York—LaGuardia.

TITLES FROM MARSH HAWK PRESS

Jane Augustine, *KRAZY: Visual Poems and Performance Scripts, A Woman's Guide to Mountain Climbing, Night Lights, Arbor Vitae*
Tom Beckett, ~~DIPSTICK~~ *(DIPTYCH)*
Sigman Byrd, *Under the Wanderer's Star*
Patricia Carlin, *Quantum Jitters, Original Green*
Claudia Carlson, *Pocket Park, The Elephant House*
Meredith Cole, *Miniatures*
Jon Curley, *Hybrid Moments*
Neil de la Flor, *An Elephant's Memory of Blizzards, Almost Dorothy*
Chard deNiord, *Sharp Golden Thorn*
Sharon Dolin, *Serious Pink*
Steve Fellner, *The Weary World Rejoices, Blind Date with Cavafy*
Thomas Fink, *Selected Poems & Poetic Series, Joyride, Peace Conference, Clarity and Other Poems, After Taxes, Gossip: A Book of Poems*
Norman Finkelstein, *Inside the Ghost Factory, Passing Over*
Edward Foster, *Dire Straits, The Beginning of Sorrows, What He Ought To Know, Mahrem: Things Men Should Do for Men*
Paolo Javier, *The Feeling Is Actual*
Burt Kimmelman, *Somehow*
Burt Kimmelman and Fred Caruso, *The Pond at Cape May Point*

Basil King, *The Spoken Word/the Painted Hand from Learning to Draw/A History 77 Beasts: Basil King's Bestiary, Mirage*
Martha King, *Imperfect Fit*
Phillip Lopate, *At the End of the Day: Selected Poems and An Introductory Essay*
Mary Mackey, *Travelers With No Ticket Home, Sugar Zone, Breaking the Fever*
Jason McCall, *Dear Hero,*
Sandy McIntosh, *A Hole In the Ocean: A Hamptons' Apprenticeship, Cemetery Chess: Selected and New Poems, Ernesta, in the Style of the Flamenco, Forty-Nine Guaranteed Ways to Escape Death, The After-Death History of My Mother, Between Earth and Sky*
Stephen Paul Miller, *Any Lie You Tell Will Be the Truth, There's Only One God and You're Not It, Fort Dad, The Bee Flies in May, Skinny Eighth Avenue*
Daniel Morris, *If Not for the Courage, Bryce Passage, Hit Play*
Sharon Olinka, *The Good City*
Christina Olivares, *No Map of the Earth Includes Stars*
Justin Petropoulos, *Eminent Domain*
Paul Pines, *Divine Madness, Last Call at the Tin Palace, Charlotte Songs*
Jacquelyn Pope, *Watermark*

George Quasha, *Things Done For Themselves*
Karin Randolph, *Either She Was*
Rochelle Ratner, *Ben Casey Days, Balancing Acts, House and Home*
Michael Rerick, *In Ways Impossible to Fold*
Corrine Robins, *Facing It: New and Selected Poems, Today's Menu, One Thousand Years*
Eileen R. Tabios, *The Connoisseur of Alleys, Sun Stigmata, The Thorn Rosary: Selected Prose Poems and New (1998–2010), The Light Sang As It Left Your Eyes: Our Autobiography, I Take Thee, English, for My Beloved, Reproductions of the Empty Flagpole*
Eileen R. Tabios and j/j hastain, *the relational elations of ORPHANED ALGEBRA*
Susan Terris, *Ghost of Yesterday, Natural Defenses*
Madeline Tiger, *Birds of Sorrow and Joy*
Tana Jean Welch, *Latest Volcano*
Harriet Zinnes, *New and Selected Poems, Weather Is Whether, Light Light or the Curvature of the Earth, Whither Nonstopping, Drawing on the Wall*

YEAR	AUTHOR	MHP POETRY PRIZE TITLE	JUDGE
2004	Jacquelyn Pope	*Watermark*	Marie Ponsot
2005	Sigman Byrd	*Under the Wanderer's Star*	Gerald Stern
2006	Steve Fellner	*Blind Date With Cavafy*	Denise Duhamel
2007	Karin Randolph	*Either She Was*	David Shapiro
2008	Michael Rerick	*In Ways Impossible to Fold*	Thylias Moss
2009	Neil de la Flor	*Almost Dorothy*	Forrest Gander
2010	Justin Petropoulos	*Eminent Domain*	Anne Waldman
2011	Meredith Cole	*Miniatures*	Alicia Ostriker
2012	Jason McCall	*Dear Hero,*	Cornelius Eady
2013	Tom Beckett	~~DIPSTICK~~ *(DIPTYCH)*	Charles Bernstein
2014	Christina Olivares	*No Map of the Earth Includes Stars*	Brenda Hillman
2015	Tana Jean Welch	*Latest Volcano*	Stephanie Strickland

For more information, please go to: **www.marshhawkpress.org**